# Letters from Henry

# Dedication

*This book is dedicated to*
*Two wonderful communities,*

*Alleyn's School*

*and*

*St. Barnabas Church, Dulwich.*

*Thank you for everything.*

# Letters
# From
# Henry

*Anthony Buckley*

Highland

First published in 2018 by Highland Books, 2 High Pines, Knoll Road, Godalming, GU7 2EP, England

ISBN-13: 978-1-897913-96-3

ISBN-10:  1-897913-96-6

Ebook ISBN: 978-1-909690-96-7


Printed in the UK by CPI Books

# *Contents*

An anticipated return.............................9

1   Any offer of hope makes a difference ............15

2   The picture may be bigger than we realise ....19

3   Are off-hand comments worth risking?............22

4   Owning the decision to make the journey ....24

5   Hopelessness in an old friend............................30

6   Being thankful, one day at a time ....................34

7   Listening to music, not noise ...........................37

8   Finishing well, one day at a time ......................39

9   The danger of despair.......................................44

10  Bravely facing the fear of failure.......................46

11  Be strong enough to ask for help......................49

12  Guard against the thieves of hope ....................50

13  Worrying can be catching ................................56

14  A little perspective always helps.......................59

15  Quotes for the school library ...........................63

16  Hope amidst the busyness.................................71

17  The blessing of sleep ........................................74

18  Hope in forgiveness .........................................76

| 19 | Forgiveness further explored | 78 |
| 20 | Patience is the friend of hope | 82 |
| 21 | Hope in disappointment | 85 |
| 22 | Hope is a team game | 89 |
| 23 | Parents: laying the Foundations | 91 |
| 24 | Parents: building hope in children | 95 |
| 25 | And yes, it is all about love | 99 |
| 26 | Letting hope fly, by letting go | 103 |
| 27 | Hope for a grieving child | 107 |
| 28 | And his mother | 110 |
| 29 | Hope in the questioning | 112 |
| 30 | Any dream won't do | 118 |
| 31 | St Paul and holding on to hope | 121 |
| 32 | St. Peter and the value of articulating hope | 125 |
| 33 | The hope that underpins all hope | 127 |
| 34 | Isaiah's insights | 129 |
| 35 | The fragility of hope | 134 |
| 36 | Nicodemus, deep down knowing what's right | 137 |
| 37 | Caiaphas, the danger of compromise | 140 |
| 38 | Mary, the value of perseverance | 143 |
| 39 | A Farewell to Matilda | 146 |
| 40 | A challenge to James | 149 |

# Contents by Recipient

| Editor | A challenge to James | 149 |
| --- | --- | --- |
| Freddie (student) | Patience is the friend of hope | 82 |
| | Hope in disappointment | 85 |
| George (old friend) | Hopelessness in an old friend | 30 |
| | Being thankful, one day at a time | 34 |
| " | Listening to music, not noise | 37 |
| " | Finishing well, one day at a time | 39 |
| Headmistress | Picture bigger than we realise | 19 |
| " | Hope is a team game | 89 |
| Mrs Jones (Parent) | And his mother | 110 |
| | Hope in the questioning | 112 |
| Librarian | Quotes for the school library | 63 |
| Major Quilter (Organiser) | Any offer of hope makes a difference | 15 |
| | Off-hand comments worth risking? | 22 |
| " | Nicodemus, knowing what is right | 137 |
| " | Caiaphas, danger of compromise | 140 |
| " | Mary, the value of perseverance | 143 |
| Martin (schoolboy) | Hope for a grieving child | 107 |
| Mary (young friend) | The danger of despair | 44 |
| | Bravely facing the fear of failure | 46 |
| " | Be strong enough to ask for help | 49 |
| " | Guard against the thieves of hope | 50 |
| " | Worrying can be catching | 56 |
| " | The fragility of hope | 134 |

| Matilda | A little perspective always helps | 59 |
| (Niece) | Hope amidst the busyness | 71 |
| " | The blessing of sleep | 74 |
| " | A Farewell to Matilda | 146 |

| Michael | St. Peter and the value of | |
| (Student) | articulating hope | 125 |
| Olivia | St Paul and holding on to hope | 121 |
| (Student) | The hope that underpins all hope | 127 |
| 2 Students | Isaiah's insights | 129 |

| Mrs Smiley | Parents: laying the Foundations | 91 |
| (PTA) | Parents: building hope in children | 95 |
| " | And yes, it is all about love | 99 |
| 2 Parents | Letting hope fly, by letting go | 103 |

| Simon | Hope in forgiveness | 76 |
| (Old friend) | Forgiveness further explored | 78 |

| Speaker | Any dream won't do | 118 |

| Teacher | Owning the decision to journey | 24 |

# An anticipated return

I think Henry would have guessed I might turn his letters into a book. Not for any publicity for himself, that was never his interest, but because he knew that this is what I tend to do. It is my way of processing and organising, of introducing and concluding. I do not know if he liked my writing. There had been occasional words of quiet approval, but he was never one to gush with superlatives and excessive compliments. Perhaps that was because he knew there was something in me that wanted him to do so, and that this something was a feeling best ignored, not indulged.

Faced with these letters, what else would I do? So here they are, put together under a title I chose, because it reminds me of that day, in his study, in his house, as the sun began to climb in the morning sky. Henry's letters, songs of the bright morning. Why 'songs' when there are none here? Because when I was younger he enjoyed turning to me and asking what background music would I give to a tree or a sunset, a conversation or a meal? He would then solemnly say "That says a lot about what you think of it." He said this final phrase so often that I would sometimes join in, and we would laugh together. Child and adult, two friends joined by a familiar joke.

I am older now, nearly thirty, but the thought of the phrase still makes me smile. As I gazed at the box of letters I knew each one would gently hold the question "James, what music goes with this?" Music behind words, songs of the bright morning.

I have kept the letters in the order he determined, which was chronological, and have kept the headings he gave them. My guess is that there were other letters he chose to exclude from this collection, and I am intrigued to know what might have been in them, and why they were left out. In any conversation one only hears what the other person is prepared to reveal.

Let me take you to a morning in May, a year ago. Or rather, first, to the night before.

\*\*\*

I thought it would be strange sleeping in the house again, more familiar to me than any other I had known, but now feeling so different, because he had died. He was not here.

It had been a long journey; I arrived late in the evening, the trains had been bad. I still had a key to the house, the same one I had been given when a child. I did not properly look round the downstairs, that could be left until tomorrow. A quick glance through the doorway of each room, as if somehow simply checking that they were all still there, seemed enough for the moment.

I went upstairs to the small room I knew so well. It did not feel so very strange after all, and perhaps the long and tiresome journey had done its work. The bed was not made, so I lay on top, hopeful that the spring warmth would be enough in the unheated house. I went to sleep.

Henry Felix-Hammond had been a friend of my parents. He had always been a person of some stature in the village, partly because of his ancestry (his family had been there for generations), partly because his private means were such that he did not have to go away to work. He was a constant but unobtrusive presence in village life, quietly interested in people and books. His most regular commitment was his weekly afternoon at the library as a volunteer.

He was a little older than my parents, and I think he had welcomed them kindly when they had moved to the village. Children do not always know exactly how their parents make friends, but for as long as I can remember, Henry was part of the scenery.

My family story had been complex, difficult, unsettled and sometimes just plain unhappy.

*An anticipated return*

Henry had opened his home to me. For me, as a child, then an adult, his house was stability and sanctuary, it was rescue and welcome. It was always there. It was the closest thing to home I had experienced. And now I had come back.

And he was gone.

The next morning I woke early, while it was still dark. I got up and went to the kitchen. There was some coffee powder, no milk or sugar, but that would be enough. The kettle was where it always had been. I made the coffee, took it into the study and looked around. There had been so many conversations in this room. Henry had been able to connect with me whether I was nine or nineteen or twenty-nine. Sometimes he talked too much, sometimes he lost track of what I had said, but the rambles and the anecdotes were kindly meant. In this room, I realised I missed him so, so, much. What had he been to me? Uncle, grandfather, counsellor, friend all rolled into one. *He had never given up on me.* Half of me wanted to hug him, half of me wanted to be terribly strong and ignore him.

The dawn began to creep around the curtains and on his desk I noticed a wooden box that I had not seen before (and I knew most of Henry's belongings as well as he had done). I opened the lid. And there was a note to me. I could just about read it in the lightening gloom.

My guess is that you, James, will be the first person who sees this (If it is someone else, please pass this on to my old friend James, who will appear before long).

James, when news spread that I was going to die, one or two people happened to let slip to each other that they still had letters I had written. Word spread, and someone had the idea of collecting some of them together. They are not of any value, but the occasional phrase may have been of some inadvertent help in reminding them of much greater wisdom than mine. They gave me the collection, and here are some of them, for you.

'Hope' is something you and I have talked about many times, even if we did not always name it. You have shown great courage in keeping going when the journey has not been smooth, in fighting when the battle has not been easy. You have always been willing to be encouraged - to receive courage - for the next step.

Continue to be encouraged, and in your turn, encourage others. Take note of the dreams that may yet matter. Travelling with hope means that you feel the destination is worth the journey. Travelling with hope shapes the journey itself. Travelling with hope means you do not travel alone.

*An anticipated return*

Thank you for all your patience and friendship.

Goodbye for now. Forgive me for what needs to be forgiven. Be thankful for the happiness you brought me. Be mindful of the blessing you can be to others.

With love, as ever

Henry

I laid this note down, next to the box, went to the window and opened the curtains. How did he know that I would be the first?

The dawn was growing and as the colours brightened I looked out at the garden. I stood there for some minutes, and then turned and went back to his desk, sat down calmly and picked the next sheet out of the box.

# Letter 1

## Any offer of hope
## makes a difference

---

*October 1990*

Dear Major Quilter,

I am pleased to hear that you are putting on a Christmas play for the village. I do not take part in amateur dramatics myself but am full of admiration for those who do. As requested, here are some thoughts about the role of the innkeeper. I realise I may have allowed my thoughts to tumble over each other somewhat further than you need, forgive my ramblings! What you will do with all this in a village play, I do not know. That is the tricky thing about Christmas, the more one looks, the more one sees; the more one thinks, the more thoughts there are to be had. Anyway, ignore or use as you wish.

*Song of the innkeeper*

*It was busy, it was busy,*
*There was no denying that.*
*People from all over.*
*One or two, excited to see the*
*town.*

*Seldom visited,*
*A name at the edge of a*
*Half-remembered dream.*

*Most were reluctant:*
*Census fodder;*
*Imposed upon.*

*Oppressed again.*

*It was busy. It was busy.*
*There was no denying that.*
*The money was good*
*and the inn was full.*
*And there was room below,*
*in the straw*

*For that last*
*young*
*couple.*

Will the audience know the context? Joseph and Mary have been forced by a remote government order to travel from north to south of their country of Judea, on the eastern shores of the Mediterranean, to the town of their ancestors. All over the Roman Empire, people similarly were walking or riding, back to their family roots. The newer towns were emptying, the old ones were filling up. And Bethlehem is old, and so many descendants of former inhabitants were arriving there. It may have seemed hopeless for Joseph and Mary, trying to find accommodation. It may even have felt slightly panicky; after all, the baby could be born at any moment. Were the promises surrounding the baby forgotten, as they went from door-to door, asking increasingly frantically whether there was space? Perhaps not, perhaps the promises were remembered, perhaps calm prevailed.

Either way, it must have been a relief when the innkeeper said he could find somewhere. Anywhere would do.

Anywhere, anything will do. When we are feeling hopeless, then anything that can bring hope is a treasured relief. It does not matter if it is the offer of the best room in the inn or a place where the animals are sometimes kept; if it means the story can go on, it is a relief.

Anything will do: it is the lack of hope that can make a bad situation feel much worse. Suffering becomes unbearable if it feels endless.

Anything will do – but only if it is positive. False hope, found in the wrong place, can worsen the situation. The hope for an alcoholic does not lie in the temporary (very temporary) flash of pleasure when the next drink momentarily dulls the pain.

The innkeeper found space for Joseph and Mary. It was not the best room, but it was enough. The story could continue. He offered hope, they received it. The offering and the receiving seem to be what mattered.

Might this be of help for the play?

Yours sincerely

Henry Felix-Hammond

# Letter 2

## The picture may be
## bigger than we realise

*October 1990*

Dear Headmistress (Miss Tyler, if I may),

Thank you for your letter. Ah, my fault, my fault; I had not realised that Major Quilter would be turning to the school for much of the cast. You must have been rather bemused when he handed the letter to you. You are right, my words perhaps were not quite suitable for the age-group, thank you for letting me know. Perhaps (but this may be wishful thinking on my part) you are still able to use something of the central point of hope given and received? Whatever you decide, I wish you well. I am glad that your pupils are taking part. Christmas is one of those events when the telling of the story is the best place to start.

How we tell a story, how we interpret it, is always an interesting question: Do we allow it to speak for itself or do we bring out particular selective themes and messages. And if we do bring things out, then what are the motives for our selections? I often have a sobering dream of Mary, Joseph, a shepherd or a wise man saying to me: "You think *that* matters?! Actually, it was *this* moment that was the big one." But what their *this* is, I do not know, the dream fades too soon.

The same question can be asked about any event: with our voices or our ears, we are continually editing, and this, I guess, is as true of incidents in home or school life as it is elsewhere.

Back to Bethlehem, might this interest the children? You may know that the ox and ass were not mentioned in the Christmas narratives; but they had been, in the wistful words of Isaiah, many hundreds of years before:

> "The ox knows its master, the donkey its owner's manger, but Israel does not know, my people do not understand."

So, whenever we see the ox and the ass in pictures or in a play, we should remember they have been included as a rebuke to us blind humans. We think we are so clever, but sometimes we miss the big picture – so big that even animals can see it.

And sometimes of course, it is not arrogance but *worry* that can blind us: we are so consumed with our own anxieties that we miss what is really going on. And we then miss the glimpses and glances of hope that might be there (and certainly were at Bethlehem).

But perhaps it is an encouragement, not a rebuke: We may be too pre-occupied to see the hope, but the hope is there. It is always there. The ox and ass remind us.

Sorry. Slightly off the point.

All good wishes

Henry Felix-Hammond

# Letter 3

## Are off-hand comments
## worth risking?

---

*December 1990*

Dear Major Quilter,

Thank you for your letter, and indeed for introducing Miss Tyler to me. I am sorry if my comments were not as relevant or helpful as I had hoped. And I can assure you whole-heartedly that my comment about the alcoholic was not in any way meant personally about anyone in the village. Purely made as an illustration.

Now, please trust me when I stress that my aside was not in any way personal, but your comment did get me thinking about remarks and responses (again, not about any one in particular, but more generally; sometimes I like to float ideas).

I realise that off-hand comments can have quite a powerful effect on me, whether or not they were intended for my ears or seriously meant at all. It is as if they can unexpectedly connect with something already going on inside me. It is as if my mind has suddenly become a call and response song. In my wiser moments I ask myself why the responses are sometimes surprisingly, even painfully, strong; I search my soul a little and see if anything needs looking at. That can open the door to new hope, to new beginnings.

Well done on the play. I thoroughly enjoyed it. You have a real gift for organising such things.

Yours sincerely

Henry Felix-Hammond

**Letter 4**

# Owning the decision
# to make the journey

*January 1991*

Dear Miss Purkiss,

Thank you for your kind letter; I am glad the nativity play went well and that the children in your form enjoyed taking part. I enjoyed watching, although perhaps our project for the new year should be to do something about the chairs in the village hall! Do you think the people who designed them ever sat in them? It is not enough to *look* good if you are a chair, you need to *be* a good chair, and that means being fit for purpose.

It is kind of you to share your thoughts with me, and kind of Miss Tyler to mention my name.

Your decision to focus in lessons on the journeys of so many of the nativity characters seems very wise to me. You are right, the choice to make a journey, whether it is a geographical, emotional, or spiritual one, is always a significant moment (think of all the stories based around this theme). Our motives might be mixed and our hands may be forced – Mary and Joseph would not really have wanted to go to Bethlehem, but an oppressive government made them. The shepherds and the Magi chose to go, but the reasons for the going came in very different ways to them. Herod refused to journey (whilst pretending that he would), and his refusal means he gets it wrong.

Allow me to add one further example that may illustrate this, and perhaps interest the children?

The baby at Bethlehem grows up and one day is found in Jerusalem. In that city he meets a person by the pool of Bethesda who, we read, "had been an invalid for thirty-eight years." Jesus asks him: "Do you want to get well?"

The person replies, noting that "I have no one to help me into the pool when the water is stirred. While I am trying to get in, someone else goes down ahead of me."

Jesus heals him and the man goes off, carrying his mat.

The religious leaders bump into the man, rather miss the big picture, and say, "It is the Sabbath; the law forbids you to carry your mat."

Jesus' opening question may have seemed unnecessary to those listening. Of course the man wants to get well! Why bother asking? But Jesus knows that the man needs to try and put into words how he feels and what he wants. His response is slightly unclear and focuses on his traditional understanding of where healing can be found; but he knows his need of something better, even if it is simply expressed as a wistful (or grumbling?) observation. He is deciding, however inarticulately, to begin a different sort of journey.

The man acknowledges his pain and frustration. Through no fault of his own, he was too slow to reach the supposed healing qualities of the pool when the waters were stirred up. Others were overtaking him. Despair can often include this feeling of being left behind. Others are overtaking us as we flounder around in the confusion of our thoughts and loss.

I need to say this gently: strange as it may seem, not everyone wants to get well. They are content as they are. Healing (especially healing of the emotions) always involves change, and that can be a challenge.

Jesus knows that the person wants to get well, is willing to make the journey, is ready to receive the hope that is being offered, and heals him.

There is immediate criticism of the man: "The law forbids you to carry your mat." And sometimes we, too, will hear voices that rebuke any desire to move to a better frame of mind: You do not deserve it, that will not work, you are breaking this or that imaginary rule by even thinking you might one day be free to walk out of this prison.

But the voice that the person chose to hear was the one that could bring healing, and he was prepared to ignore those other powerful, destructive voices, and he chose to pick up his mat, and walk.

It is a gift to be able to hear the voices that bring hope, not despair. And it is a gift to be the voice that is able to bring hope, and woe-betide us if we choose to be that voice that brings despair: Stay on your mat, keep on being emotionally paralysed; you have no right, it is dangerous, to think any different.

I am sure you are very good at bringing hope to the children in your class. Perhaps that is the most important part of a teacher's job.

Yours sincerely

Henry Felix-Hammond

## How had he been perceived?

I smiled. I imagined the conversations in the school staff-room: "I have had an extraordinary letter from Felix-Hammond, the chap who lives at the house at the end of the village green. No wonder the Head passed him on to me: couldn't cope with any more herself, I would think. As old as the hills and can't stick to the point. Rambles all over the place."

But he had not really been all that old back then. Amid the ramblings I wondered if Henry had been trying to say something to the teachers as well as the children. He always enjoyed scattering thoughts, and never quite knowing where they would land, or where they might spring up. And I wondered whether Major Quilter really did have a drink problem (or was I falling into his trap of assuming motives to Henry that he may not have had?).

And when you ramble, you get to see new places. And he meant well. He always meant well.

I suddenly felt protective. I hoped the teachers' chuckles, if there were any, had been kindly, not contemptuous.

I picked up the next letter.

## Letter 5

# Hopelessness in
# an old friend

*March 1991*

Dear George,

I am sorry that you are feeling low, and please forgive me that I have not been in touch for some time. Thank you for saying hello at the Christmas play (went rather well, I thought, well done Major Quilter!). Thank you for writing now, I know that making contact is not always easy when the skies seems very dark.

I do not know all the details of what may be troubling you and perhaps there is no need for me to do so. But I am guessing that underlying it all, what is making it all seem so bleak, is the possibility that you are wrestling with the understandable questions: *Will things ever get better? Will I ever feel happy again?*

So, please forgive a brief and inadequate response until I know more about your situation: I would encourage you to think quite strongly about hope. It seems to me that the very existence of the word 'hope' is part of our acknowledgement that our world is not perfect. If it were perfect, we would not need hope.

George, life is a struggle, a battle, a journey across uncertain terrain where the weather is out of our control, and hope is a vital companion in the journey. Can we define hope as the belief that it is always worth carrying on the journey, for reasons we may not know or understand, and that these reasons have roots deeper than anything we may be currently experiencing? Or is that much too verbose?

Hope is to be spread through all we do, like the tapestry fabric that holds the threads. It is at the core, not an optional extra. So when you are feeling particularly flat, allow yourself to think, even with a smile, if you can: "Ah, it is for times like this that hope is especially needed! Where might I find hope now? What different things have given me hope in the past? What can I reach for?"

If nothing springs to mind, write to me again, and challenge me to come up with some answers. But I cannot resist making one suggestion now:

Set yourself a couple of small targets for the day. Nothing grandiose, nothing noisy, just little things that you will manage, and which may do some good. I once saw this poem:

> *When despair chases*
> *and hunts me down*
> *And nearly has me, and is so close*
> *I will not surrender yet.*
>
> *When images of loss and pain*
> *Are given to me, each time I wake*
> *I will turn my eyes away.*
>
> *And will set myself some simple tasks*
> *And give myself some real dreams*
> *To reach my bed alive*
> *To help a friend to smile*
> *To turn and face the sun*
>
> *And cruel despair will lose his prey*
> *And fading away, his voice will drop*
> *To almost nothing at all.*

Interestingly, my old friend, when we get the simple tasks, the little things, right, the big things have a habit of working out, as well.

But the turning our eyes away from those confused images of defeat and loss and pain: that is not easy, even when those visions are patently ridiculous when brought out for detached scrutiny. That is not easy. I know that so well myself.

Enough from me, be in touch as you wish

Henry

**Letter 6**

# Being thankful, one
# day at a time

*March 1991*

Dear George,

Yes, the overwhelming feelings can block out so much else, I think this was what I was struggling to say at the end of the letter. "Encircling gloom" indeed. But we need to keep it at bay. Hope has to do with looking out and looking up. Life is sometimes so busy, or our minds become so full (not quite the same thing), that we feel that we do not have time to note the "Kindly Light." One of the important side-effects of living each day well is surely that it gives us a rhythm and a space to think.

You will already have developed a routine, we all do; my guess is that you clean your teeth at roughly the same time each day? Perhaps have meals at roughly the same time - beginning, middle, end? May I suggest that we mutually commit, as old friends, to ensure that a time to be thankful is included in our rhythm? When thankfulness becomes a habit of mind it is interesting how positive the world can become; one begins looking for the good things – that smile, this moment, that rainbow - as opportunities to be thankful, and that changes how we feel.

Do you remember those chats about Paul's letters? "Be thankful always", he says to the Thessalonians. And when addressing anxious Philippians he stresses the need to offer prayers "with thanksgiving". He did not see thanksgiving as an added extra, more of an essential backdrop to everything else we may be doing.

I am starting to think that there is a great hope-filled power in being thankful. The appreciation of what we have, the counting of blessings even when they seem rather hidden. And surely, if we are in the habit of noticing and appreciating what is good, we are likely to feel that tomorrow there will equally be something worth noticing and appreciating. Who knows, perhaps the Giver will give more?

There is something about being thankful at the beginning and the end of each day, something about the rhythm of night and day which seems to be of value, physically and emotionally. There is so much in our modern lives which means we end up blending work and rest, light and darkness. There is wisdom in the separating out, so the picture becomes a mosaic rather than a splodge. Didn't Jesus talk about concentrating on the needs of the present? Saying, perhaps with a wry smile, that we should let the worries of the day be enough, that tomorrow will bring a whole new set?

Sometimes poets and writers re-imagine a life using the imagery of the day (Remember how we used to sing 'Lord of all hopefulness' at school?). There is that same sense of time being not simply a succession of minutes, but rather a pattern or a curve. A symphony is not only a string of notes; there is a beginning, middle and end, and the player adjusts the mood and expectation accordingly.

Thus it might be worth considering how you mark the seasons in each day, and build in thanksgiving, expectations, reflection, making amends, prayers as you wish.

As ever,

Henry

## Letter 7

# Listening to music,

# not noise

---

*March 1991*

Dear George,

Briefly this time: My hymn quotations reminded me of music. Do you still play the piano so beautifully?

Ponder this idea: There is a difference between noise and music. Our world is full of noise, and our minds are sometimes full of noise: lots of shrieking sounds, or a couple of unpleasant, cruel voices, filling us with worry or fear.

When you played (especially the Beethoven!) I forgot the noise, it was driven away. I heard the music. Is it any surprise that nearly every significant political movement for change has included songs and music?

What is going to be the good melody today? Will we notice the subtle, supportive harmonies?

Attend to the music and shut out the noise, all that shouting and all that emotional crashing about that our minds or society seem to enjoy.

Look for the beauty...

Henry

**Letter 8**

# Finishing well, one
# day at a time

*April 1991*

Dear George,

Very true: some of the songs we hear are sad ones. And some of them are indeed full of regrets, mine certainly are. So, if hope is about looking to the future, how do we deal with the past? Forgive the trite question (and my even triter thoughts in a moment), but I wonder if this is always one of the central themes of moving forward? And, of course, the older we are, the more past we have to deal with.

Do you remember that meeting we went to together, all those years ago? They were bright days, were they not? We heard a talk about the rhythm of each day, especially about ending it well. We were reminded about the discipline of a daily pattern of life, and how this helped people in previous centuries cope with much more anxiety and uncertainty than most of us ever experience, at least in this country.

At the end of each day: Facing up to, reflecting upon, what has happened and then going to sleep with a clear conscience. As I said before, there is perhaps something here about thanksgiving, honesty, reconciliation, and hope: the awareness that we land well in order to help us take off once more for new adventures.

And you used to have this G. K. Chesterton quote on your wall?

> *Here dies another day*
> *During which I have had eyes, ears, hands*
> *And the great world round me;*
> *And with tomorrow begins another.*
> *Why am I allowed two?*

George, today is nearly past, a new one dawns tomorrow. Can we recapture, can we still glimpse, the sense of wonder?

May I offer two thoughts?

The first thought involves breaking things down a little, into seven themes:

* Being honest, not over-estimating nor under-estimating what is whirling round.

* Being thankful for what has been good.

* Admitting to hurts done to us.

* Admitting to mistakes we have made.

* Admitting to sins we have committed, and seeking forgiveness if we have not already done so.

* Planning to do something kind, noble or just plain right. There is real power in morality.

* If you still believe in God, give it all to him when you pray.
  He is outside time, so he can bless the past as much as he can the present. He can bring good things out of the past even when (to our eyes) so much seems to have been lost.

The second thought is this:

We may need to look forward before we look back. Where do we want to be in a day or a week's time? How do we want to be feeling? Imagine ourselves there. And then, from that perspective, look back, what would we have needed to do between now and then to get from here to there? What would have been the markers on the road? Perhaps there are changes that need to be made, attitudes adjusted and behaviours altered. Things to do.

In answering this we may then have a clearer insight into what *in particular* from our past may be slowing us down, what needs to be dealt with.

Keep in touch

Henry

## The kindness of George

I remembered George. He was an old college friend of Henry's who had died a year or so ago. Sometimes when I was staying during the summer holidays he would visit for a day or a weekend. He had been friendly enough whilst not quite having that easy way with people that Henry did.

These were personal letters, I felt I was intruding by reading them. But Henry had left them for me, and George had sent them back to him, presumably knowing that they may end up being read by someone else. Perhaps Henry had touched on some things that George had felt were important enough to be heard by others, whatever his own vulnerability and exposure might be.

George must have been a good man, I silently affirmed him. Perhaps that was why he and Henry got on so well. I hope his darkness had lifted.

I looked back at the box.

# Letter 9

## The danger of despair

*November 1993*

Dear Mary,

I am delighted you are enjoying the history course, and well done to the library for running it. I like libraries, as you know when you used to call in with your mother after school. I am glad the council has found a use for that extra room at the back.

I do not know as much as I should about mediaeval thinking so will not be able to help you with your essay, but I am pretty sure you are right: I think that despair was always considered one of the most dangerous of moods by the great thinkers in those days? Perhaps this was for two reasons:

First, from their point of view, it is an expression of a lack of faith in God to make things better, whether on earth or in heaven. For them, the only rock-solid reason for any hope at all was the character and purposes of God. Thus, if a person despaired, they were rejecting this traditional understanding of the nature of God.

Secondly, the very practical reason that despair can bring grumpiness and even unkindness. If we are planning a treat on Saturday, we are likely to walk with a spring in our step on Friday. We are likely to enjoy what is to be enjoyed, and even smilingly put up with what would not normally be much fun. Who minds preparing for a party? We clean the tables with a smile, our mood is brighter, and we will want to help others in the cleaning party to feel good, too.

But if there is only despair about Saturday, if there is to be no treat, then Friday may feel like trudging through treacle. Cleaning the tables feels a waste of time. No reason to smile, no reason to attend to the needs of others.

Despair was to be resisted as much as possible; hope was to be embraced, and strengthened by meditating on all that is good. Perhaps more on this in another letter.

I hope this may be of some small interest, if not much help with the essay.

Very best wishes

Henry F-H

**Letter 10**

## Bravely facing the

## fear of failure

*November 1993*

Dear Mary,

Thank you for your kind reply, you are very right – sometimes despair can be triggered by a sense of failure.

May I become embarrassingly over-dramatic and quickly pen a speech, to be declaimed in the high Victorian style as they fondly imagined the heroic Saxons to speak? Do not read it too loudly in the hushed confines of the library if I am not there on volunteering-duty that day.

"Ha! Tired, boring old dragon, named Exaggerated Failure Maximus, I see your game. You want to crush me with regrets and shame. See here, what weapons I have to hand, and with these I will fend off your blows, and will protect the hope in my heart. I hold the sword of truth, thus I will admit to what I have done wrong, but I will not exaggerate my faults. And

I wear the cloak of mercy; there is mercy in this universe and I travel under it. And my gauntlet reaches for the good memories, and grasps hold of the assurance of those who continue to hold me in affection and respect. Creature of despair – depart from me! I walk in hope and will not be distracted. There is work for me to do."

Forgive the tone! I was never any good at drama (this is a continual disappointment to Major Quilter, I am sure), so I have to practise on you.

But you will see the point. We need to see despair as an enemy that wants to breed pointlessness and lethargy. The old thinkers viewed it as an evil because it is destructive and takes away trust, in oneself, in friends and in God. When we despair, we are likely to do less good than when we have hope. Do not see despair as an inevitable feeling against which we are powerless. See it as a foe that must be beaten back.

And when the old dragon comes waddling back, as periodically it will, then each time we must go through the disciplines: working through how truly justified our feelings of failure might be, apologising or forgetting as need be, remembering that some things we do get right, and working out where we need to go from here.

Keep things in balance,
keep things in perspective.

Best wishes,

Henry F-H

# Letter 11

## Be strong enough
## to ask for help

*December 1993*

Dear Mary,

Again you are right, and I am justly rebuked – sometimes we feel so despairing that we lack the strength to fight back at all. That is where help should be sought from those who can give wise counsel.

But perhaps I am not completely wrong? – It takes strength and courage to seek such help. Perhaps that is the first battle to be fought and won. There are others who are willing and equipped to fight the dragons for us. The best knights always saw themselves as part of a fellowship. Remember that the Round Table had *many* knights, not *one* knight.

All the best

Henry

# Letter 12

## Guard against the
## thieves of hope

*February 1994*

Dear Mary,

Thank you for your letter and no need at all to apologise for the slight delay in the reply. You are juggling two issues, your studies and your support for the friend. I can imagine you advising her wisely, very wisely indeed – life can indeed feel very complicated in our muddled age, and I am thinking of her very much, and of you, as you kindly walk with her.

And I am now beginning to piece together the reasons for your interest in hope It is typical of you that you were hesitant to say that you were spending time considering your help for someone else, as well as, incidentally, having to write an essay.

Perhaps rightly so, our good deeds should not be proclaimed from the housetops, but it is equally right to affirm the importance of what you are doing by being alongside her. Your role as a companion during these difficult days will be treasured by her (and no doubt by the angels) for longer than we may guess.

In terms of her beginning to consider what perhaps are the 'thieves' of hope, may I offer the following very brief thoughts?

It is well-worth the time for her (you rightly did not name her; may I call her Marilyn?) to consider if there is something in particular that has stolen the hope. It may be a disappointment or a worry, a sadness or a wound, or a combination of things. Babies and toddlers are full of hope; if Marilyn feels that her hope has been taken away, then the 'when' and the 'by what', or even sometimes, sadly, the 'by whom' are good questions to ask. There will not always be clear answers, but asking the questions can begin to point to the right journey ahead.

Forgive a prosaic first suggestion: a common thief of hope is tiredness. It is simply more difficult to feel full of bounce and vigour if physically we are tired. Ask her about her sleep.

And her eating. The right amount of energy is really, really, important.

Perhaps she feels she has been badly let down? She may, deep down, be wondering if she can ever trust anyone again, or herself, or the world, or God (if she believes in God). A chat about trust, what it means, why we need it, how to grow it, whom to trust, may yet be helpful.

And lots of honesty. If she has been hurt, especially if she has been hurt by people close to her, then at some point she needs to name those feelings quite clearly, certainly to herself and perhaps to someone else.

Another thief may be a memory of, or fear of, letting people down. To come to terms with the truth that sometimes we disappoint others, as they sometimes disappoint us, is not always easy. Perhaps a reassurance that she is still needed, has a role to play, and that it is not in anyone's interests for her to leave the stage, or to fall silent, may be of some help.

Repeated supposed 'failures' can steal hope away. I included the 'supposed' because our definition of 'failure' may be worth a look. I knew someone at school who was tearful if he got 99%, while others were delighted if they got 55%. The pass-mark was 45%.

If Marilyn feels she has failed in many things, then it is worth her checking what she really means by 'failed' and why that bothers her. There may be good reasons, but she needs to be honest about the roots and validity of her expectations. And whether the targets set for her, by herself or others, were sensible: (My ambition may be to play cricket for England – that is not going to happen, so is that a wise target to have? Have I failed if I have not achieved it?). Whose voices does she listen to as she ponders what truly is success or failure?

Is Marilyn worried about the way she looks? Again, worth checking whose 'voices' she is hearing if she is pondering her appearance. Perhaps gently remind her that people do not change the world for better because they are good-looking, they change it because they are good. Everyone who loves her thinks she is beautiful anyway; life is too short to worry about those who don't love her in the first place. Sorry to be blunt on this one. I am ugly. No one really knows what Alfred the Great looked like. Churchill looked like a wrinkled baby. I am not interested in what Marilyn looks like, much more interested in what she can do and how she thinks.

And, connected with this, a tendency to compare can be a thief of hope. Whatever happens to me, if I always compare myself with others, I am unlikely to feel content. It is always the wrong question to ask.

And (this is one of the nastier thieves of hope): when someone makes it clear they think we are useless, it can be like a punch in the stomach. It is as if we become emotionally breathless, not able to think or feel anything else until the shock passes and we can breathe normally again.

Speaking of age, the fear of running out of time can steal hope away. We think that unless 'it' (whatever 'it' may be) is achieved within a certain timetable, usually of our own artificial making, then we are finished. But the people who change the world simply get on with doing what needs to be done when they are able to do it.

A good rule of thumb is this: if the thoughts lead down a pathway of despair, then this is a thief, not an angel, speaking. A good voice will leave you feeling hope-filled, even if challenged. The thieving voices will take away your self-esteem, and leave you with nothing. They do not want the best for you. They are deceitful and manipulative. Ignore them or, if you really feel you need to fight, get some strong allies alongside.

Imagine that Marilyn is guarding her home, and is conscious that there are thieves close by, seeking to steal her hope. She will wisely be aware of the vulnerable doors and windows, the entry points, and take particular care that they are defended, and that the right questions are asked before someone comes in.

And her doors and windows will be different, Mary, to yours or mine. Let us all be aware, and on our guard.

Perhaps the biggest thief of hope can be the feeling that there is no ultimate meaning or purpose. To keep that thief at bay, one has to decide the reasons why things matter, why it is worth carrying on. Has she thought about her philosophy of life, what she believes and why she believes it?

My apologies Mary, this is probably much too long (and equally much too short, I have only raised possibilities, not addressed them). Ignore as much or all as you wish; whatever you do, I will be thinking of you, and dear Marilyn.

Very best wishes, and well done for all you are achieving.

Henry

PS It is interesting how sometimes our studies and real life can intersect.

**Letter 13**

# Worrying can be catching

*February 1994*

Dear Mary,

Forgive me another letter so soon. You have been on my mind and I cannot resist this brief follow up. Do remember that if Marilyn has a tendency to worry, then it might be helpful to explore whether a parent or close adult was, or is, also prone to worry.

Worry is catching, especially from parents, and there are three reasons:

* First – the child realises their beloved parents are not as secure and stable as expected. That is inevitable at some point, but if worry is the parents' continuing state, then the world can feel much less secure for the child.

* Second – the child mimics the parent's reactions. If the adult reacts with excessive worry to a situation, then that will be the learned behaviour that the child will absorb.

\* Third – the child grows up believing the world must be a terribly scary place. If their big, strong, beloved parents are fearful, then who can be safe?

I am exaggerating for the purpose of brevity. I throw these thoughts out, make of them what you will.

Of course, some things really are worth worrying about. But purposeful concern, determined to find a solution or a means of coping if the problem is insoluble, is different from excessive worry being the constant, dominant, default response.

Healthy concern is like an appropriate blast of trumpets at the right moments during a concert. But if all the music is one long blast of trumpets, then it is no longer a symphony, just a noise.

Best wishes, as ever

H F-H

---

### Being able to be available

I wondered who Mary was...

Clearly someone in the village, given the reference to Major Quilter. And a person who for some weeks had occupied Henry's thoughts. There was a sense of focus, of stepped-up commitment and attention. Perhaps this was how he worked, throwing himself in one direction and then, when the task had come to an end (perhaps she stopped writing to him?) he would withdraw to the edges again.

Was that ever difficult for him? Emotional investment is costly, and part of the cost can be the sense of being left behind as the other person moves on. It was not the time to ponder whether I had moved on at different moments, and how Henry had felt about my periodic withdrawals, but one day, perhaps I should.

As well as wondering who Mary was, I wondered how she knew Henry was worth writing to. Did people talk about him in the village? Perhaps the quiet figure helping in the library and walking around had been appreciated more than I realised. Perhaps word had spread that the response would always be kind.

I went back to the box, and another name appeared, here was one I knew, and I smiled, with memories of golden afternoons in the garden, of picnics and games, of sunshine and laughter.

# Letter 14

## A little perspective
## always helps

*July 1994*

Dear Matilda,

Thank you for your kind letter. It was lovely to see you, thank you so much for coming over.

You knocked over a pot-plant. I do not agree that this means you are a 'clumsy fool' nor that your visit was 'a disaster'

It seems, my favourite (well, my only, but I am truly deeply fond of you) dear great niece, that you are in danger of over-reacting, what I think could be called 'catastrophising'. You knocked over a pot plant; this does not mean that your entire life from birth to now has been a complete failure, nor that the angels are turning their back on your future with a resigned 'I knew it would come to this' sort of sigh.

You knocked over a pot-plant. Your aged, pompous, forgetful, pedantic, irrelevant great uncle can handle that. The wild but ordered universe can handle that. God can handle that. The question is, dear Matilda, can you handle that?

There are three dangers of catastrophising, and I think you are at more risk from the first two than the third:

The first is that we become robbed of hope. We dwell so much on our small mistakes or sins (there is an important difference here, which is worth considering, but perhaps another time) that we lose the big picture. We do not recognise the gifts that we have and can use for the good of others; we do not look forward to the new day because we become convinced we will mess it up.

The second danger is that we become so terrified of doing anything wrong that we do not try to do anything at all, or we go to enormous unnecessary lengths to cover things up whenever we think we might have made a mistake.

The third danger is that we may begin to treat others in the same way: She pushed in front of me in the bus queue? She is full of evil. He dropped a plate while washing up? He is an appalling person not worthy to be a friend of mine. He forgot to buy the soap? The lowest circle of hell is rightly reserved for him. It sounds silly as soon as we put it into words, but we should always be on guard against this subtle temptation to catastrophise faults, with ourselves and with others.

With love. Come and visit again soon, and you can knock over as many pot-plants as you wish.

Henry

## *Where was I in this?*

As a child I sometimes wondered what it would have been like to have been related to Henry, to have been family, perhaps to have been a great-nephew. I remember wistfully wondering if he felt differently about Matilda than about me, or (in my worse moments, and even as a child I knew this was not a good emotion) whether she was given better presents than I was at Christmas.

But I had liked Matilda a lot, that point of stability through many awkward years, and my affection easily crushed any possible envy. And deep down as a child, on better days, I knew that Henry cared for me very deeply, whatever the label. There was compassion of course, although he never pressed, and we only talked about my dysfunctional family if I wanted to (which was not often), but there was also affection. He liked me. Children can sense if an adult likes them. And I didn't find it easy to think people liked me.

My reverie slowed down and then came to a sharp halt as I came to terms with the realisation that I still don't find it easy.

I stood up and looked at the floor, twisting my fingers behind my back. I think I remained like that for some minutes. Not moments, minutes. And then I decided to go back to the box.

# Letter 15

## Quotes for the
## school library

*September 1994*

Dear Mr Symmons,

I am glad the school has a librarian, it is such an important role and I wish you well. Thinking about it: I am simply glad the school has a library, and then of course especially pleased that someone like you is there to help and suggest. There is something restorative in the feeling of sitting surrounded by books - all those books, all those words, all those characters, all those authors. Titles written to describe or entice. So, thank you for the letter, I am very happy for Miss Tyler to have passed on my address. My involvement in the library world is much more feeble than yours, and I applaud you.

I am honoured that you would like some thoughts for your display, and the request to link them to historical figures makes it an even greater challenge! 'Village notable' is too big a title for me; how about simply 'friend of the school?'

I have decided to suggest some riddles; as you can see, I am a very bad poet, but I do think that riddles can be quite fun and attempting them echoes our Saxon heritage. The children could come to you and see if they have guessed the answers. Here they are; forgive me if I miss the mark, I do not know what the pupils will have been studying and I am conscious I have probably been rather off-beam with my suggestions to date for the school. It is hard for us outsiders really to know what is going on inside a classroom. The teachers are the experts.

Here is the first:

*Alone, hard-pressed, retreating,*
*    the tired king lacks all;*
*Hoped-for risings failed,*
*    replaced with fall on fall.*
*The enemy is gaining ground,*
*    with triumph in his eyes;*
*If royal light is crushed to dust,*
*    the hope of England dies.*

*Forget the songs and minstrel tales,*
*　　forget the later myths;*
*Forget it if the cakes are burned,*
*　　forget all else but this;*
*It all comes back to holding on,*
*　　regrouping once for all.*
*In the silence of the lonely hour,*
*　　will he stand or fall?*

Would the children have heard of Alfred the Great? In the winter of 878 AD, after yet another defeat, he fled to a hiding place in the marshes of Somerset, and decided, one more time, to keep going, to contact his soldiers, and to keep fighting. The Danes were defeated, Wessex was saved and seeds were sown for a rich crop of English identity, culture and power.

* * *

*'All shall be well,' she writes.*
*　　'All shall be well.'*
*Words easy to quote,*
*　　Words easy to say*
*But she lived through years of*
*　　Black Death hell*
*And still she can hope,*
*　　And still can she say:*

*'All shall be well, and all shall be well,*
*And all manner of thing shall be well.'*

This is Lady Julian of Norwich, who, as a child, had seen the catastrophe of the Black Death (She also happened to be the first woman in England successfully to publish a theological book). Reflecting on her life, she felt she could still live the hope: "All shall be well".

* * *

*When death amidst the Oxford flames*
*Began to hallow martyrs' names,*
*"Light a candle" was the cry*
*Of brave men knowing they would die.*

I wonder if martyrs, of whatever background, ever have a pang of hopelessness. Might they ever wonder if their sacrifice is for nothing? Perhaps this is a temptation for all who seek to carry out good deeds. Can we be sure these deeds will make a difference? Perhaps a candle is lit whenever a good and honourable sacrifice is made. I do not mean the supposed 'sacrifice' indulged in by ignorant, selfish, and hate-filled terrorists. *Motives matter.*

Anyway, this is Latimer and Ridley, in 1555, not forgetting dear old Cranmer, who lost his nerve and later found it again.

***

*A nonsense dream to stop the trade,*
*    To make us paupers yet*
*Our country needs, deserves, the cash.*
*    Our destiny is set*
*If not us, then others would*
*    – At least we treat them right –*
*You may make this speech for thirty years:*
*    You'll never win this fight*

But he, and others, did. William Wilberforce just kept going. And the slave trade came to an end. Those who mocked and feared were wrong.

*** 

*Through quiet wards, the lamp is seen*
*And beds are ordered, neat and clean*
*The mud and grime fades far from mind*
*And tears grow still, through care so kind*

Florence Nightingale, bringing hope, planning and an example that would change the world.

I'll keep thinking, let me know if more would be useful. I wrote these when I needed to be inspired by braver and more hope-filled people than me; the trying to express all this in riddles was an attempt to find the right words and tone. Perhaps you could suggest to your pupils that, when they are trying to sense or express, hold or glimpse, something important, that they have permission to try poetry as well as prose.

We need more poets (and much better ones than me).

Yours sincerely

Henry Felix-Hammond

### Perhaps we only ever see a part, never the whole

I paused again, rubbed my eyes and got up. A walk round the garden would be nice. I knew where the key to the back door was kept, made another coffee and in a few minutes I was walking down the patio, mug in hand.

I do not know much about flowers and could not remember how all this had looked, what had been where in which flower bed. There was a general memory – I think roses had been there and tall daisies here? But I had not been good at the details, and as a child remembered nothing except to keep the ball away from the windows. I suppose we remember what we need to, but sometimes it would be nice to remember more.

Hidden seeds doing their work in different patches of soil. Henry's breadth of letter-writing had been hidden from me. Why shouldn't it have been? There was no reason for me to know about all his contacts; but I felt a small pang that I had not asked him more about what he did, or how he was feeling. We often seemed to end up talking about me.

But the regret was replaced by the realisation that this was how he had chosen it to be. He was quite private, and good at deflecting.

I had not expected all the religion in his letters. He, I think, had sometimes gone to church but seldom talked about it. He clearly took it seriously, or would not have referred to it so much.

Nor the poems or riddles. I remembered one poem, which he showed me with his usual laugh, pointing to a page in the village magazine: "They must have lost an advert this week so were rather desperate and had to fill in the space with this!" It was about harvest, I think. "They say I only write doggerel" he smiled, "but I don't know what that means, so I write, anyway."

The fresh air was good to feel, but my shoes were getting damp and it was time to get back to the study.

And there was another one to Matilda.

# Letter 16

## Hope amidst the busyness

*October 1994*

Dear Matilda,

Greetings dear great-niece! Work seems very busy for you at the moment? Thank you for your letter in the midst of it all. Occasionally feeling a little flat is perhaps not unexpected; busyness can be a serious enemy of light and hope, indeed it can be an enemy of pretty nearly every good thing, of everything which is peaceful and trusting. We become fearful that only our busyness can make things safe, and thus our hope becomes focused on our ability to run around and do lots of things. But this apparent achievement is short-lived and unsatisfying.

Did I ever read you this poem?

*The devil called a meeting*
  *- a kind of training day -*
*Setting out the game plan,*
  *for tempters to obey.*

*"Humanity's the target.*
    *Emptiness we sell.*
*Come on boys let's at 'em*
    *– Let's really give them hell!*

*"Keep them busy, keep them at it.*
    *Keep them occupied.*
*Never give them time to ask*
    *if they are satisfied*
*Let them trust in idols,*
    *created in their minds,*
*Not crude and wooden statues,*
    *but deeper, subtler kinds*
 *'How do I look? Do I succeed?*
    *Do people notice me?*
*Am I tall and rich and bright,*
    *and perfect as should be?'*

*"Keep them stressed out,*
*keep them wound up,*
*keep them petrified.*
*Never give them time to ask*
*if they are satisfied.*

*"Keep them from good pleasure,*
    *from wanting to be free.*
*From seeing the potential*
    *of all that they can be.*
*From friendships, fun and laughter,*
    *from joy at each new day.*
*From searching for the purer light,*
    *that drives our lies away."*

May I suggest that you consider what it is you *need* to do today, and what you really *want* to do today, and do as little as possible of anything else? It is amazing how much time we spend doing things we do not want or need to do.

The secret is to know ourselves well, and our calling well.

Your loving great-uncle

Henry

**Letter 17**

# The blessing of sleep

*October 1994*

Dear Matilda,

If I may say, a really good question: Can a lack of sleep be another enemy of hope?

Yes, I think it can. When we are over-tired we tend to do work less well than we should, which can make us feel flat, and we can lack energy to notice the positives because we are investing all we have in just getting through the day.

And what to do? Well, there's a lot of good advice around, but my counsel would be simple

Work out how many hours you need: not necessarily what you have currently got used to, but what medical wisdom, practical experience and good common sense would say your body needs.

Go to bed in time so you will get these hours

Good sleep is cumulative, so stick to the routine. Put a string of good nights together, then a string of strings.

Notice what spoils your sleep. What are you eating, drinking, reading and watching beforehand? And if it remains a problem, see your doctor.

Above all, realise that this is a priority. If you sleep well, most other things can be tackled.

I do not know if you are asking on your behalf, for a friend, or simply in general. If it is you, dear Matilda, sort it out soon. Sleep really matters.

Love from

Henry

## Letter 18

# Hope in forgiveness

*March 1995*

Dear Simon,

Thank you for the lunch and for allowing me, inviting me, to visit your family.

That moment of joy and relief, when I realised you had forgiven me! One can tell it in a hundred ways, perhaps especially in the openness of the smile. Because if you had not forgiven me, then something would be held back, the eyes would have been more distant. And of course the invitation in the first place was rather a clue, but still I could not be certain until I heard it clearly. And your kindness in knowing my need of this, and of taking me aside and to say those words – thank you.

You have forgiven me. I do not deserve it. I suppose, by definition, forgiveness can never be deserved. Mistakes can be justified and thus excuses, in some way, can be 'earned', but sins need forgiving. I know that neither of us use the word 'sin' very much, but I must say it does seem to cover pretty well what I did. It is a blunt, clear, me-centred word and I had been selfish, cruel and greedy, and you forgave me.

I don't quite know what that cost you, the hurt you had to soak up and let go. I suppose, if I thought about why you did it, there would be something here about you caring for the person so much that you did not want the misdemeanour to stand in the way. I feel very humbled by that.

Thank you, thank you, thank you.

I do not see as many people as I used to. Things tire me in different ways than they once did. I spend a little time writing rather clumsy replies to various letters. So the lunch was a treat, and I was refreshed and nourished, physically and emotionally!

Very best wishes to you all,
and thank you again

Henry

# Letter 19

## Forgiveness further explored

*April 1995*

Dear Simon,

As soon as I posted the letter I thought: 'He will come back to me on this, he always had a good mind and he will push me further!"

I agree, we don't give much time these days to think about forgiveness: what it is, what it looks like, why it matters, what it means to forgive, to be forgiven, to forgive oneself. Perhaps schools should have lessons on it; after all, they have lessons on how to avoid financial debt; spiritual and emotional debt is surely just as serious an issue.

Here we are then, some further musings in reply to your wise thoughts. And it is typical of you to deflect attention from your own kindness by pondering more general themes.

Does the other person need to say sorry? I am sure they do, for their own health; I don't think they need do so for us to offer forgiveness. You and I both share the same reference point, we are duty-bound to consider what Jesus would have done. And his "Father forgive them, they know not what they do," from the Cross itself, implies that he wants people to be forgiven even when (at present, at least) no contrition is shown.

But, I must say, it makes it so much easier when the person does say sorry, however that is expressed! Perhaps there is something here about being careful not to confuse our frustration with the lack of an apology with our hurt at the sin itself? These are two different emotions which should be handled in two different ways.

I do not think that forgiveness always means an immediate cry of 'let's go on holiday together'. Divine forgiveness may work like that, but I am emotionally rather more fragile and confused. If I have been hurt badly, I can forgive the person for the act, whilst still being very wary of the person and their ability to hurt me, especially if I am not sure how remorseful they are. Again, it is about separating the different emotions. The sin can be forgiven, the hurt caused may need substantial recovery time. And if the sin involves a break of trust (as most do?) then the trust will take time to rebuild.

Forgiving oneself? So hard to do. Perhaps it helps if we remember that a good way of treating ourselves is to imagine that we are a good friend. How would we treat them? We should treat ourselves the same way. Part of living what Jesus meant when he said: "Love your neighbour as you love yourself," is to see what life looks like if we switch it round, that we love ourselves as we would want to love our neighbour.

And, as C.S. Lewis puts it: "I think that if God forgives us we must forgive ourselves. Otherwise, it is almost like setting up ourselves as a higher tribunal than Him."

At the heart of it all (for those of faith, at least) is coming to terms with what it really might mean that God has forgiven us. Incredible words from Paul in the eighth chapter of Romans: "There is therefore no condemnation for those who are in Christ." No condemnation, not from anywhere. To know we can be forgiven and that we can forgive provides such a strong emotional foundation and great cause of hope.

And, finally, I agree very much with what you say about current culture: in these days of mass-media, of rumour and swift judgments, of pantomime villains and violent words, the theme of forgiveness in society becomes ever more complex, and clear thinking ever more needed.

And it is very difficult for a community to talk sensibly about forgiveness if it has not talked sensibly about sin. Or if the church is weak (either through choice or through being marginalised) in declaring the forgiveness of God. If I hear clearly that God has forgiven someone, it makes it a little harder for me to refuse to forgive.

And, of course, any talk of God's forgiveness reminds me that I need it more than most, and that helps me to pause before I run to judgment against others. It also (can I say this reverently enough?) reminds me that in this case not only Simon has forgiven me, but God himself has forgiven me... so, if I may say, when you kindly decided to forgive me, you were standing on holy ground...

And those glimpses of holy ground always give hope. They can do no other.

Thank you again.

Henry

# Letter 20

## Patience is the
## friend of hope

---

*July 1995*

Dear Freddie,

It was very good to see you when I came round for lunch. I am sorry it has been so long, entirely my fault, and it was very good to catch up again. Thank you so much for the chat; I am thinking of you very much as you wait for news from the college. I hope it works out for you, but these weeks of waiting can indeed be rather a trial.

But as soon as I say that, I hear the voice of your father challenging me! I think that is why we got on so well all those years ago, he would hold me to account for sloppy language and I always enjoyed that. I can imagine him asking me what I mean by 'trial.' And, knowing Simon, he would also remind me of the Tertullian quote "Hope is patience with the lamp lit." By definition, hopes are not immediately fulfilled (if they always were, there would be no need of them). We therefore must work out how we do the waiting. To hope well means learning to be patient well.

We spend rather a lot of our lives in waiting, whether it is for potatoes to boil or the right job opening, for news of a diagnosis or for a relationship to be healed… or indeed for the answer to a college application.

Waiting in itself is not necessarily enjoyable. If it were, we would not have to learn the discipline of patience. And patience is indeed something that needs to be learned, babies are not born patient.

Choosing to be patient means that the waiting can become a blessing not a burden. To cope well with being bored is a great skill: to be able to create pictures in our minds, ponder acts of kindness, or imagine new adventures. Impatience can breed a grumpiness (perhaps a fear?) about the passing of time; it can lead to selfishness and frustration, unnecessary distractions and temptations. When the long-awaited event finally appears, we are not in the best mood to receive it, and may have caused harm on the way.

So dear Freddie, perhaps it is a trial in the old-fashioned meaning of it being a test. I am sure you will pass the test, and wait patiently with imagination, equanimity and good humour.

If you have a moment, let me know what the news is, when it arrives.

Best wishes

Henry

## Letter 21

# Hope in disappointment

*August 1995*

Dear Freddie,

I am so sorry the news was not good. And I remember that you were especially pinning your hopes on this one. Thank you for kindly letting me know – so much harder to share a sad update than a happy one.

There is very little I can say to bring comfort. I feel for you very much, because so many times I have tried for new roles or positions and the answer has been 'no'. I am not blithely going to say that something will turn up (although, to be honest, deep down I think it will, but that is not the presenting issue right now).

May I suggest three things?

* Do not let your unsuccessful applications lead you to think you are an unsuccessful person. One of the few things we can be sure of about heaven is that St. Peter will not be interested in what university you attended. You are a wonderful, much loved,

person who at the moment has not got to college. That last phrase is a small part of your story, it does not define you.

* Forgive the intensity of this: I am genuinely deeply fond of you, and always have been. My respect for you is not diminished one iota by this news. And that will be true of all your genuine friends.

* Keep hopeful. Think about what the future may look like, and be excited and challenged by the possibilities. Repetitive disappointment can pretend to be strong enough to crush our hopes and dreams. Stand up to it, put it in its place, and be excited about tomorrow.

Enclosed is a small gift, not very much I am afraid, but perhaps something to help you have a little treat. It is important to be gentle on oneself, to spoil oneself a little, when these things happen. When it is raining it is okay to have a nice umbrella.

All the best and lots of love

Henry

## Different people's places on the stage

It was time to stretch my legs again, I got up and looked around the study. Perhaps it was here that these letters had been written. Areas of Henry's life, fellow-characters with me on stage with him, but I unfamiliar to them and they to me. There are many others in the play; a person's life is never simply a dialogue and certainly not a monologue, nor is it always obvious whose are the most important and influential voices. We may think a character is listening only to us, but they rightly will equally be in touch with others.

I had not realised about the failed applications. Henry either wore his disappointment lightly or had found it too difficult to admit the failures. I was hit with a wave of how fond I had been of him and how I had never told him how much I admired him.

He was always so skilfully self-deprecating, I remembered one of his favourite sayings: "All I am is the chap who brings on orange segments at half time for the players, but I always drop a few on the way. Bit clumsy, really." And now I wondered if that was a cover for – something, but I was not sure what.

I had not met Freddie. I wondered what happened to him.

# Letter 22

## Hope is a team game

*October 1995*

Dear Miss Tyler,

How nice to hear from you again and all good wishes to the school.

I agree, hope is a concept for communities as well as individuals. And this is such an important part of leadership: to help the school (or any organisation) feel that it is on a positive journey. The hope then becomes an infectious virtue, newcomers catch it, visitors sense it.

Thank you for the kind invitation, I would be delighted to come and talk to your staff. In the meantime, may I suggest that it is worth looking out for the encouragers in your staff, and ensure their voices are heard? The moaners should never be allowed to take a grip (and it is interesting how often they do).

As it is for individuals, the need for a sense of identity and purpose for a community is very important. There is then the issue of how you discover, name and express what the community stands for. You and I will both know of people like X, who make some bold declaration about love and peace from the podium while behind them the employees are smiling bravely through gritted teeth, bearing the scars of X's earlier, private, cruel words and decisions. Values are to be lived continually, and, if need be, perhaps then also occasionally mentioned. If they do not speak for themselves, there is not much point in speaking of them at all.

But I know you are not so foolish to fall into that trap. My advice would be to talk to as many people as possible who are *not your natural allies;* see what they say about what hope and purpose means in your school, and build up from there.

Perhaps the most important team in a hope-filled school is the invisible team that does not come through the school gates, but which profoundly shapes those who do. It is the family that lies behind each child.

Best wishes

Henry

# Letter 23

## Parents: laying
## the foundations

*October 1995*

Dear Mrs Smiley,

I am glad the Parents' Association is going well, and congratulations on becoming the Chairperson. Thank you for your letter. I understand that Miss Tyler has mentioned that I sometimes have things to say about the word 'hope'!? I feel it is a case of mistaken identity; I am not sure I have ever been a shining example of a hope-filled life, to say the least, but I will leave that for another time.

Hope for parents? For rather obvious reasons, I don't think I am the one to ask. I am not an expert and have no direct experience. But it is very interesting, and to be commended, that the Parents' Association wants to consider hope, I think it is one of the most important issues in parenting, and indeed in our society. What is a child without hope? And if parents are not hopeful, then that can be difficult for a child indeed.

I start with the following assertion:

Children are born wanting to love their parents. They therefore want them to be happy. As time goes by, they realise their parents (being real people) are not always happy. This is a difficult but important step of development for the child.

Forgive me for being blunt: When a parent unconsciously or explicitly blames the child for their own unhappiness, they risk sowing confusion: children may start thinking: "I love my parents, I want them to be happy, but it is me that has made them unhappy." They pick up messaging like 'I could have had that job, or lived there, or taken that opportunity, *were it not for you.*' 'If you had not been such a difficult baby, I would not have had to leave your mother.' And the child feels so sad and so responsible. Now, you and I will know that these accusations are completely unfair, but the child will still half-believe them.

And then there are the times when the child realises that the parents sometimes make each other unhappy. Children learn to cope with this too, but if it is continuous and unpleasant it can be heart-breaking as well as confusing. As a child might say, or think, or feel:

> *My mum and dad are beautiful,*
> *     and that's because they're mine.*
> *You may think they're rather odd;*
> *     you may think them strange*
> *The things they say, the clothes they wear,*
> *     they have their little ways*
> *But I think they are beautiful,*
> *     and that's because they're mine.*
>
> *They don't treat each other so,*
> *     – I find this hard to grasp –*
> *The damning words come flooding out*
> *     and they don't seem to see*
> *That when they hurt each other,*
> *     they're also hurting me.*

Why I am starting with this? Because true hope is based on seeing things as they are, and one part of reality is remembering that children want to love their parents. If we consistently, deliberately, ignore or crush their needs, then eventually some of the love may die. But they do not want the love to die; they do not really mind if we make mistakes, and they do not mind at all if we have to say sorry. Children, of all ages, are very good at knowing that today is a new day, a new chapter. They want to make it work as much as we do.

Perhaps more so.

Yours sincerely

Henry Felix-Hammond

# Letter 24

## Parents: building
## hope in children

*October 1995*

Dear Mrs Smiley,

I cannot remember exactly what I wrote last time, but I am sure you are right if you say there may be room for something a little lighter! And I am very willing to offer these quick thoughts for your next letter or speech to parents. Please include in an introduction that they are simply points to get people thinking; they are not definitive, they are incomplete and clumsy musings.

* Showing your child that there is hope in the world...

* Respect yourself. Being a parent, or being a responsible adult for a child, is one of the most important callings we can be given. We are complex and imperfect people living in a difficult world, and it is sometimes all a bit of a struggle. Being too

hard on yourself if things do not go quite
to plan does not help you, nor the child.

* Say nice things to your child.
  And say nice things about other people,
  otherwise your children will not trust you
  when you say nice things to them.

* Try not to sound cross with your child.
  There may be times when you need to, but
  not many. Save the cross voice for if ever it
  is truly, honestly, needed. And afterwards,
  ponder why you felt it was.

* Look at your own anxieties;
  consider where they come from, whose
  voices you are hearing, and whether you
  are expressing your anxieties helpfully or
  unhelpfully.
  Children watch, constantly. They will
  be watching how you respond to others
  in need before they decide how much of
  themselves they can risk trusting to your
  response to them.

* Don't say it was more difficult in your day.
  It wasn't. It was different.
  So you are on a learning curve to
  understand their world, and they are on a
  learning curve to understand yours. Mutual
  humility and respect underpin good
  communication.

* Don't pretend you have all the answers.

* Allow lots of time doing normal things, washing-up, shopping, playing together. Allow space for conversations to grow.

* Do not pressure your child to 'open up' and tell you everything. If they want to, they will. If they don't, they won't. If you are concerned, and feel they ought to talk to someone, contact someone (school/counsellor/doctor) who can help from another angle.

* 'Disappointed' is a very destructive word. Your child wishes to please you more than they (or you) realise. You can be sad if they do something wrong, but try not to be disappointed with them as a person.

* Do not try, consciously or unconsciously, to mimic your own parents and their upbringing of you. You can learn from them, but you are not them and your child is not you.

* Likewise, you do not need to measure yourself against other parents in the playground. You are helping to painting a unique picture, to grow a unique plant, to write a unique symphony. Competitiveness is the wrong tool to use.

* Do set routines (children feel safe with boundaries) but be flexible and understand that the routines change as the child grows.

* Do explain your thinking: "Because I say so" is a weak arguing position, and your child knows it is. So do you.

* Look after yourself, emotionally, mentally, spiritually and physically. Your welfare is important to your child. They will understand trauma and illness, but will find deliberately self-destructive behaviour confusing and hurtful.

* Attend to your own hopes, but not at the expense of the hopes of others. Remember that all real love involves sacrifice. If you have not sacrificed something in your life for the sake of your child (or a friend, for that matter) then you may need to ponder what you mean by love.

Sorry again to be blunt. Let me know if I can help explain these better.

Very best wishes

Henry

# Letter 25

## And yes, it is all about love

*October 1995*

Dear Mrs Smiley,

Yes, it is all about love (it is *always* all about love). And we need to remind parents that this is the way through. I would extend this to all adults. I think all of us, without or with children, have some parental responsibility to the next generation. This is one of the reasons why exploitation or abuse is so appalling: the adult is refusing to play their proper role. It is not the worst reason, which of course is the horrendous damage done to the child, but such role-confusion is a useful warning sign. When the adult ceases to be the responsible adult, then that little bit of the world becomes out of joint, and disaster can creep in through the gaps.

Part of parenting can be unwittingly developing the habit of a constant sense of failure: 'Second in the ballet exam – must be my fault as a parent.' 'Ten minutes late back from a party? That is not how Fred next door would have behaved, so what am I doing wrong?' We can catastrophise too quickly.

They love us and we love them, but we may be unsure as to what love looks like; we need to remember that love is about relentlessly wanting the best for the other person. Part of this will be setting boundaries. Love is not about indulging the child's every whim. We need to think carefully as to what is the best for them, lest we are simply processing our own insecurities. Many cultures hold on to the intuition that 'it takes a village to raise a child.' Sensible—I am always uneasy when a parental figure is not listening to the heritage of wisdom that is so widely available. St. Paul writes that:

> "Love is patient, love is kind. It does not envy, it does not boast, it is not proud. It does not dishonour others, it is not self-seeking, it is not easily angered, it keeps no record of wrongs. Love does not delight in evil but rejoices with the truth. It always protects, always trusts, always hopes, always perseveres."

And then points out that anything done in love will last for ever.

This is rather encouraging. Perhaps he is right.

*May I share a little story?*

Marilyn looked at her life and despaired. She had not achieved what she had hoped. She was sometimes lonely. She tried to get back to sleep but her mind was racing: What if? Why didn't I? If only?

It was still very early in the morning, and she drifted into a dream. And in that dream someone came to her with a case. "Here is your luggage for the journey," he said.

"Thank you," said Marilyn, "Let me carry it." For the case seemed large, heavy and cumbersome.

The man laughed "It is rather heavy, and look, there are plenty more." And Marilyn turned and saw a trail of people, all carrying bags and cases of all sizes.

"Why I do need all these?" said Marilyn "What is in them? What is it all about? Have I done something wrong?"

The man smiled. "You packed them. You do not need them, but they may bring you joy. Every kind act you ever did has been kept and stored, remembered and honoured. Every kind thought, every kind word. They are here. They are held forever."

"Why?" asked Marilyn.

"Because they are marked with the touch of the one who is love. And nothing that is of him can be lost. They have his seal. You are not to despair, you are to keep loving. There is more to do."

So the parents can be hopeful, because love will always have an effect. It is never wasted. Never.

I hope the evening goes well for you all.

Best wishes

Henry

# Letter 26

## Letting hope fly,
## by letting go

*November 1995*

Dear Mr and Mrs E…,

Thank you for your letter and I am glad the evening at school went well. I fear that I may have been clumsy in passing on my words and am sorry if they caused upset for you. Indeed, I truly believe and accept that you feel that "you know what is best" for your daughter. If any of my quoted words caused offence, then no doubt there are things we can all learn from them and our reaction to them.

And I am very sorry to hear of the pain caused by her disobedience and tantrums, and the despair that often must be felt. Parenting is one of the most difficult jobs in the world; you have my admiration and my sincere good wishes.

Letting go: Is there something about allowing hope to flourish that means we must not cling too tightly? As you know, we cannot really control the outcome of every situation by wrapping the event or the person so closely that they cannot breathe and live in their own right. Perhaps hope always works like this: in order to grow and begin to be fulfilled, it needs its own light, its own space. And thus we adults need to release, not smother.

And this is so difficult, especially when we feel we love the person so much, and all we want is the best for them; but, and I say this very gently, we do not reliably know what is the best for them, we do not know all ends, we do not know all eventualities, we are not them (we find our own motives difficult enough to fathom, let alone anyone else's). Perhaps a key thing we can do is to keep watch on ourselves, to try and understand ourselves a little more, as we gently watch their story unfold, too.

I have known some people who have been so keen to avoid thinking about themselves that they have focused solely on the imagined needs of someone else. And that did no-one any favours.

I am going off on a tangent, and should draw to a close. I think of you so much in this continuing pain and worry. Keep the hope going, and I will be thinking of you and your daughter very much; thank you again for writing.

Very best wishes

Henry Felix-Hammond

## Needing to be honest about how all this feels

I paused. Many different emotions: Would I admit that there was slight anger at Henry that he had included these ones for me to read, knowing what echoes they might bring? But this was mixed with curiosity that he had wanted me to see them. And there was pain: so much here struck deep chords in me. And appreciation: his kindness to me when I was a teenager was informed by an understanding that what I was going through really mattered. These ones had been included because he would have felt I needed to read them. What was on his mind?

What about his gentle, but robust, response to Mr and Mrs E. who then had returned the letter for this collection? I could not tell if it was his or their marker-pen that had redacted the names. It was gracious of them to return it.

This was all very close to home for me, as Henry would have known it would be. I would have liked something lighter after this. But that is not always how things are.

# Letter 27

## Hope for a grieving child

*January 1996*

Dear Martin,

Your form teacher, Miss Purkiss, tells me the sad news that your grandmother has died, and that perhaps you would like to hear from me?

I feel very honoured by that, thank you. I enjoyed visiting your class last week and think I remember you. Were you the one sitting in the middle on the back row? And I think you excellently answered that question about the king who burned the cakes? And whether it matters if it is a story or history?

Now, I need to say that we all react in different ways when someone dies. This is fitting – all of us are different and all our relationships are different. What I am going to say in this letter are thoughts that have helped me; they may not all help you, and you will have your own helpful thoughts. Perhaps you might tell me one day some of your good ideas.

The first thing I would say is that it is right that you are sad. Whether you are crying on the outside or the inside, the fact that you are sad shows that you love your grandmother very much, and that is a good thing. You may also be feeling sad because your mother (it is her mother who has died, I think?) may be upset. And because you love her, you are sad for her, too. Whenever our sadness comes from love, it is a healthy, perhaps even a holy, sadness. So do not worry about being sad. It may be terribly painful, but it is not wrong. At all.

Secondly, it may be helpful and rather fun to bring to your mind good memories of your grandmother, the times when she smiled and when you smiled, the times of just being with her, the things she enjoyed and the stories you remember her telling. As the weeks go by, different memories will come to mind – enjoy them, share them (perhaps with your mum?) – and always remember that you would have given your grandmother much joy. You made her happy (grandchildren do that without really trying, but no doubt you did try, and this is to your credit) and that is a good and important gift that you gave her.

Thirdly, be gentle on yourself and anyone else close to you. It is important that we are kind to ourselves when we are going through difficult times.

And lastly, remember that lots of people believe in heaven. I certainly do. And therefore I feel that death is a comma, not a full stop; it is the end of a chapter, not the end of a story. That, even among the tears, can be rather exciting to think about, but I don't want to make this letter too long, so I will stop here.

With all good wishes, and I am sad for you, grief is a big thing, and rightly so.

Mr Felix-Hammond

# Letter 28

## And his mother

*February 1996*

Dear Mrs Jones,

Thank you for your kind letter; I enjoyed writing to Martin (if I may say: I am sure he is a wonderful son, and a credit to you) and I continue to think of you, him, and all the family in this sad time. It must all have been such a shock.

I know what you mean about not wanting to ask the 'why' question yet. At the moment the grief is too raw.

May I share this poem with you? I heard it once at a funeral.

*There may come a time when we will ask*
*The Why that brought us here,*
*A time when questions rich and deep*
*May fall on listening ear.*

*But that can wait,*
*Yes that can wait*
*And that can wait some more*

*For now,*
*The tears flow smooth and plain*
*They speak of love and speak of him*
*And hold him close once more*

*They speak of heart, of memories*
*of joys and hopes and dreams.*
*So let me cry, and let me smile.*
*And let me hold him close.*

*The rest can wait*
*The rest can wait*
*Just let me hold him close*

Be in touch if ever you wish, but
please do not feel you have to.

Yours sincerely and
with deep, deep sympathy,

Henry Felix-Hammond

**Letter 29**

## Hope in the questioning

*April 1996*

Dear Mrs Jones (Jane, if I may?),

Please do not feel guilty that you took a couple of months to write. There is no hurry at all (and if you had decided not to write at all, that would have been completely fine, too).

Thank you for your letter, and I note that perhaps now is indeed the time for the 'why' to be asked.

May I speak plainly? This is one of those questions that bring together the emotional and the intellectual, the heart and the mind. If I speak too bluntly, please do not take that for a lack of feeling.

Nearly every death is a deep sadness to someone else, whatever the age, whatever the cause, and rightly so. The philosophical problem of suffering is as much an issue when one person dies peaceably in a bed as when hundreds die in an earthquake. Some suffering is caused by our cruelty and greed, but most deaths are the result of the way our world works. Illnesses abound, germs do their work, bodies deteriorate, hard surfaces damage me if I fall on them. We are physical beings in a physical world. A feature about our existence is that every living thing dies. Death is inextricably woven into the fabric of the strange, beautiful, colourful and confusing tapestry that we call life.

So, the straightforward answer to the 'why' is because this is how it is. This is how the world works. Often the 'why' is more focused – 'why now?' 'why her?' and, again, this goes back to the way we work as natural creatures. Different things happen to us, and no person's life span is predictable with any confidence; it would be a very different world if it were, and one that may be more difficult for us psychologically to inhabit than we think.

You may know that I speak from a Christian background, and I do not know if you share that worldview, so forgive me if the next part feels irrelevant to you. For the Christian, every death is somehow strange, every death is a tragedy, because all death is a reminder that the world is not in its best form yet, that it is stained with suffering and incompleteness. Hence Jesus weeps at the funeral of Lazarus. Hence the big promises of heaven. Paul writes that creation itself is waiting for its healing and restoration. John writes that there will be a new heaven and a new earth, and no more death.

Why things followed this course, I do not know. But I would rather be able to moan or shout at God for allowing it to be so, than resignedly accept the effects of the movement of mindless molecules. I would rather beat my fists against the chest of a God who is weeping with me, than have no-one to wail against.

If I were to say: "Ah, Jane, the exact reason why your mother died now is this or that or the other" you rightly would not believe me. There are some things we simply do not know. And, it would be an extraordinary power to know why everyone dies when they do. Can we really imagine living in such a world?

We live in a world which includes death as part of its scientific make up. I cannot quite grasp what a world would be like if it did not. But there is something in me that keeps reaching out for an existence that is free of death, which somehow works even though I cannot comprehend how. Perhaps you and I were made for such a world as that. Perhaps that explains the strangeness and sadness of death. And as soon as we take these feelings seriously, we are beginning to ask the big questions…

All that is merely scratching the surface of where our minds may go as we consider these things. But I am so conscious that our heart needs to be spoken to, even more so. I do not want to extend this letter, but may I briefly say something I mentioned to Martin: We are relational beings, and if our relationships are healthy, then we feel the loss deeply. It says so much about you that this hurts so much. The tears, inside or outside, speak of love. Death only hurts because we love.

And thus, it is an honour to be in touch with you.

With very best wishes

Henry F-H

## The risk of writing letters

Parenting and grief? What did Henry know about either? And then a memory came back of something my father had once said to my mother: "All things considered, he has coped very well." But my father had then moved on to something else, and I had never known what were the things that could be considered.

I caught myself thinking about my parents' painful and bitter separation, and wondered how Henry had felt about that. Watching old friends tear themselves apart. I turned back a few letters. Had he looked at me when I was a child, playing in the garden, having hot milk at the kitchen table, and wondered if I ever felt: "when they hurt each other, they're also hurting me"?

It was quite strange thinking about what Henry thought of me. It made me think of me, too. I wondered what I had been like. I wondered what I am like, now.

And again my thoughts turned back to this: Was I right in thinking that these letters were chosen deliberately for me? Probably others had sent theirs back, but Henry had selected only the ones he wanted me to see. This collection on the table was not only about him, this was about me. But perhaps also it was about others, as yet unknown, whom he thought might end up reading them if I did put them in a book. When we send words into the air we never quite know where they will land.

Had Mrs Jones written back? How did Henry cope with not always knowing how his letters would be received? Could he be sure that I would be receiving them in the way he intended, whatever that may have been?

**Letter 30**

# Any dream won't do

---

*June 1996*

Dear Mr Trevors,

I enjoyed the evening at the village hall; thank you for coming along to give your lecture to our little community supper club. I am an old man and am sometimes blunter than I should be, so I hope these words do not give offence.

In a nutshell: I think you missed a crucial point.

In your "Words to inspire" you were right to encourage us all to aim high, to dream big dreams. What would have been helpful is if you had encouraged us to think carefully about how we know which dreams to follow. I find the dreams I have after a day walking the hills somewhat different to those I have after enjoying too much wine and cheese. Whose voices should we be listening to, as we consider which dreams we should be pursuing? Most of us have several voices in our heads, all suggesting we should do this or that or the other. Unless we know which voices we should be attending to, how can we know which dreams to follow?

Some voices will be giving us inappropriate goals which we will either never achieve or, if we did, they would make us deeply unhappy. It is simply not enough to say: "Any dream will do." Would you say that to a mad dictator? I am sure you would have the intellectual and moral integrity to challenge their dream. Not all dreams are the same.

If we are to be hopeful people, we need to be realistic. I thought your talk would have been helped by a section on how we can find reality, so that we can dream well.

Please see this letter as a compliment. You are an inspiring and skilled speaker; that means all the more you should be thoughtful about what you say. With gifts come responsibility.

Thank you again and I hope you take these words in the spirit with which they were intended.

Yours sincerely

Henry Felix-Hammond

# Why keep a critical letter?

The sentiments were not a surprise, Henry had frequently (and, to be honest, rather repetitively) made his feeling clear about the intellectual inadequacies of the 'any dream can do' school of thinking. What caught my attention was that Mr Trevors, whoever he was, kept the letter and returned it when the word went out that a collection of letters was to be made. Did he return it to show how grumpy Henry could be? Or to show how incisive and wise Henry had been? I did not know Mr Trevors' motives, and Henry would have known I would not have known. So much behind these letters was hidden from me, and I am someone who likes all the loose ends to be tied up.

I glanced down at the box; I should be finished soon.

# Letter 31

# St. Paul and

# holding on to hope

*January 1997*

Dear Olivia,

I am glad that you are enjoying college, your parents kindly keep me in touch with how things are going. Although you must feel it is all very different from the village, people are much the same anywhere, and in time you will probably build good friendships there as you have done here. Don't worry if you don't, or even if you need to wait until later. You will come across the right people in time.

Thank you for your letter. That sounds an interesting essay you have been set and I spent longer in the library today than usual, looking through the shelves once the borrowers had gone. It is a long time since I have read St Paul's second letter to the Corinthians. I sometimes quote from the thirteenth chapter of his first – it is so good about love (and, rather interestingly, possibly written out of frustration with his readers – it is intriguing what can sometimes come from an angry pen). If you have been asked for something about hope from the second letter, then I would go for this from the fourth chapter:

> "Therefore we do not lose heart. Though outwardly we are wasting away, yet inwardly we are being renewed day by day. For our light and momentary troubles are achieving for us an eternal glory that far outweighs them all. So we fix our eyes not on what is seen, but on what is unseen, since what is seen is temporary, but what is unseen is eternal."

There is so much in this, but perhaps a key point is that it is worth attending to the 'inner you' as well as the 'outer you'. The 'outer you' matters, and things happen in your life that will affect how you look, feel, and think. Your outer self needs to be attended to, but if you spend one hour in front of the mirror, and one minute pondering whether you can be kind to someone today, then your values are out of balance. Paul was sometimes distressed and oppressed, grumpy and discouraged, things happened which he would have preferred to avoid, but he kept attending to his inner life, and so he could say: "therefore we do not lose heart." And, paradoxically, he attended to his inner self by looking outwards. Paul saw himself as a citizen of heaven, and so a priority was to honour, and grow in, that citizenship. It is as if a cricket player finds herself practising with friends in a large park, and around her lots of people are playing football. Whatever the external noises may be, and however strong the sense of group pressure, she wisely continues to practise her cricket. The targets espoused by the world around Paul were not the same targets that he held dear.

Scoring runs is different to scoring goals. Paul was stubborn and focused, and was very careful about whose agenda he was following.

And was very conscious of his weaknesses, and his tendency to be knocked back by events. Earlier he writes

"We are hard pressed on every side, but not crushed; perplexed, but not in despair; persecuted, but not abandoned; struck down, but not destroyed."

So, dear Olivia, I think I would begin with the idea that Paul and his friends knew that the world could be very difficult, but they clung on to the bigger picture, the stronger dream, to see them through. Do you know the book of

Habakkuk? Paul would have known these words by heart:

> "Though the fig-tree does not bud and there are no grapes on the vines, though the olive crop fails, and the fields produce no food, though there are no sheep in the sheepfold and no cattle in the stalls, yet I will rejoice in the Lord, I will be joyful in God my Saviour."

Note the 'yet'. That's the spirit, that's what Paul is aiming for, that's where he finds his hope.

Best wishes

Henry

# Letter 32

## St. Peter and the value
## of articulating hope

*January1997*

Dear Michael,

So Olivia got Paul and you got Peter?! The village is very proud that you are both there, and studying happily.

In my translation 1 Peter 3:15 reads like this:

> "Always be prepared to give an answer to everyone who asks you to give the reason for the hope that you have. But do this with gentleness and respect, keeping a clear conscience."

Perhaps five points from this, sorry this is brief (slightly rushed today).

* Peter, in choosing one word to summarise the belief of his readers, chooses 'hope'. That, for him, is the quickest way of describing the loving, positive faith that he shares with them.

* He expects them to have reasons for this hope; it may take time to think these through, hence the need to 'be prepared.'

* Others will be intrigued by their hope, and are likely to ask questions. There is something very attractive about hope, and people will wonder where it comes from

* Our explanation is to be gently given. Peter does not want us to be crushing or contemptuous. Our reasons may be strong, but we are to use that strength kindly. Because we respect the other person, as they are. Made in the image of God and fellow-traveller through this difficult world.

* Finally Peter wants his readers to have a clear conscience (and it is interesting that he includes this). How can I truly explain the love and mercy and hope of God to a friend if an hour before I have been shamefully cruel and deceitful? Our behaviour matters.

In haste, but very best wishes

Henry

# Letter 33

## The hope that underpins all hope

*February 1997*

Dear Olivia,

You are right – my comments about Paul implied too much about gritting teeth into the gale and not enough thinking about heaven. Of course, that hope is the Big One (as Paul would have been the first to point out).

I once visited an old lady in hospital. She was about to die. She was lying flat on her back, staring at the ceiling. When she realised I was in the room she said, clearly and directly. "I don't want you to tell me I am going to get better. I am not, I am going to die. I want you to tell me about glory."

And so we talked about heaven.

The point that struck me was that she did not want any false hope. If I had said "I am sure you will feel better tomorrow, and we will have you home in no time at all" she would not have believed me (what do I know, anyway? I am not a doctor) and her trust in me would rightly have lessened.

Olivia, I rather like thinking about heaven, and I suggest you think about it, too (I am conscious I am drifting away from the essay). With our modern fear of death, contempt of religion and frantic attempts to prolong physical life as long as scientifically possible we seldom have serious conversations about what heaven might be like, whether it exists, and if it does, what difference that might make to our earthly existence.

Perhaps all our earthly hopes are echoes of this ultimate eternal hope?

All good wishes

Henry

# Letter 34

## Isaiah's insights

---

*March 1997*

Dear Michael and Olivia,

Sorry, saving time by writing to you both! Thank you for your kind responses.

Yes, Peter and Paul, these two tough, strong-minded first-century figures, often under immense pressure (and both ending up being killed for their beliefs), love talking about hope. Here is Paul to the Ephesians:

> "I pray also that the eyes of your heart may
> be enlightened in order that you may know
> the hope to which he has called you."

Interesting use of the word 'enlightened', implies that thinking hopelessly is a result of being overshadowed, of not seeing things clearly.

And, for both Peter and Paul, hope is something with a specific cause, they believe that the promise of life in all its fullness is to be found in relationship with the risen Christ. Why can they feel hopeful, despite intense persecution? Because they are on the winning side.

Earlier in the letter Paul talks about the presence of God's Spirit being like "a deposit guaranteeing our inheritance". Later he will say,

> "We are God's handiwork, created in Christ Jesus, to do good works, which God prepared in advance for us to do."

And that sense of calling, that there is a good task, that especially fits us, is a powerful force for contributing to a positive and hope-filled life.

Paul and Peter would have known this passage from Isaiah chapter 40 very well:

> "Do you not know? Have you not heard? The Lord is the everlasting God, the Creator of the ends of the earth. He will not grow tired or weary, and his understanding no one can fathom. He gives strength to the weary and increases the power of the weak. Even youths grow tired and weary, and young men stumble and fall; but those who hope in the Lord will renew their strength. They will soar on wings like eagles. They will run and not grow weary, they will walk and not be faint."

Here are five themes that might be worth considering, forgive my childish delight in beginning them all with the same letter!

* *Realism*

  Whatever our age, whatever our apparent strength, we will become weary. The writer uses the age-old literary device of parallelism (emphasising one truth by saying it twice using different words - Tired/weary; stumble/fall). Let us be honest: our strength is limited; acknowledging this can be liberating.

* *Reference point*

  There is only one source of eternal strength; there is only one who will not fade. As so often in the Old Testament the point is made that this God is the one God; this is not one of many tribal deities, this is the God of the ends of the earth. He is the everlasting God, having no beginning or end and therefore his strength does not fade or decay. His understanding is too deep to fathom, so we need not be surprised if not everything makes sense to us.

* *Reminder*

  But we sometimes forget this and need to be reminded: "Have you not heard? Do you not know?" It may be good to ponder:

What squashes out, or causes us to forget, the nature of God?

* *Reliance*
  And so, the hope is to be in him, because no-one else can fully deliver. What does this trust look like? There will be something here about handing over our worries; about trying to live the values of the Kingdom, about trusting that his voice is the right one to hear. There will be something about patience, holding on, doing the right thing, even when the good outcomes are not immediately present, of keeping on loving.

* *Reassurance*
  And then we will soar like the eagles. Not simply keeping going, trudging along the path, but we will fly. Although physically our strength will fail, spiritually we will not grow weary, we will not faint – there are glimpses here of the big promises of eternal life.

I think one could argue that these are some of the thoughts that lie behind Peter and Paul's world view?

Best wishes

Henry

## *Why was this so unfamiliar to me?*

This was all a bit heavy. Henry in preaching-mode was not what I was used to. But perhaps he was teaching, not preaching. After all, he was not insisting that Olivia and Michael believed this.

There was something here about wanting people to understand, and being prepared to take them further. I had never heard of Habakkuk and only very vaguely of Isaiah (was he sometimes quoted at Christmas?).

And in so many of these letters there were religious references. Why hadn't Henry talked about these things more to me? And at the same time another question came to mind: Why hadn't I asked him?

It was rather a relief to glance down and to see that he was back to an old correspondent.

## Letter 35

## The fragility of hope

---

*May 1997*

Dear Mary,

Thank you for your letter, it was lovely to hear from you again. And thank you for remembering the thoughts about hope and thieves of hope.

You are right to add another: a person can be a thief of hope. Most of us have the power sadly to do this to someone else. When we so skilfully undermine, when we crush with words or actions, when we stand in the way and block out the light. We may think that we have come out on top, that we have made the big show, the killer statement, but in trampling on others we have died a little ourselves, and our hope is a stunted selfish affair. Real hope is rich and broad and seeds hope in others. It is not a tree that grows on its own.

Mary, may I speak plainly, I am wondering if someone has tried to take away your hope. That is a serious thing for me to say, and I apologise if the thought causes you pain; I merely say what is on my mind. I am then wondering if, understandably, you have become a little defensive and over-cautious, and the idea of reaching out again for hope feels too complex, too threatening. What is left of your hope needs treasuring and protecting, and space to flourish once more.

Don't worry about answering if you prefer not, but know I am thinking of you deeply in all this.

A child once sent me this, after I had visited his school.

*When hope is bruised,*
*    give time to heal;*
*When hope is squashed,*
*    Give space to breathe.*

*It is a sapling tree, a gentle plant,*
*    Seeming strong one day*
*Looking weak the next,*
*    Needing sun and rain, time and care.*

*When hope is bruised,*
*    give time to heal;*
*When hope is squashed,*
*    Give space to breathe.*

I think that is rather good. There is a tendency, when hopes are dashed, to rush in and interrogate the hope: why were you not up to the job? Why did you crumble so easily? These questions may well be helpful at some stage, but there is wisdom in taking a deep breath, in allowing the tender shoot to uncurl from the floor where it has been flattened.

How to be gentle on the hope whilst it slowly lifts itself from the floor? I think the same way we are called to be gentle on ourselves more of the time than we perhaps realise. Check that the sleeping and eating are going well, find time for rich, harmless pleasures, don't compare yourself with others. And spend time with people who not only speak words of hope but who seem to embody hope. Hard to put into words, but you will know what I mean.

Best wishes. Be gentle on yourself Mary, I think that is rather important.

You are much loved.

Henry

## Letter 36

# Nicodemus, deep down, knowing what is right

*September 1997*

Dear Major Quilter,

Thank you so much for your kind letter, and it was a pleasure to see you in fine action in the cricket on the green. If I may say, the way you ran between the wickets was impressive indeed! You are healthier than ever. And I am sure an inspiration to others

Yet another play?! Your energy never fails. I like the idea of various Easter tableaux round the village next spring, and it is kind of you to ask for suggestions. May I mention one character, seldom mentioned, who perhaps would be worth including?

He is Nicodemus. I wonder what he felt on Friday morning? Perhaps news did not reach him until then that Jesus had been arrested. Caiaphas the High Priest would perhaps have included some of the Sanhedrin in his scheming, but my guess is that he would have been hesitant to let Nicodemus know, nor anyone else whose loyalty could not be guaranteed. The Sanhedrin, the ruling council, were the big players, while still under the authority of the occupying Romans. Caiaphas thought he had control, and he nearly did. But there were loose cannons (forgive the anachronistic reference) among them, and Nicodemus was one. Nicodemus had made it clear in an earlier meeting of the council that he was against the execution.

Which was an interesting moment of courage, because earlier he had only dared to go and see Jesus by night, perhaps because he was frightened of what other people thought of him. Jesus did not seem to mind that at all. (I don't think Jesus minds nervousness very much, he is not one of those insecure speakers, liking the volume turned up to help keep the ego going. A bruised reed he will not break, as dear old Isaiah would say.)

Anyway, something seems to have clicked on Friday. Perhaps it was the appalling trial or the horrific execution, Caipahas' manipulations or Pilate's abnegation of responsibility. And so he had enough. This man once so nervous he could only see Jesus secretly (and this was early, before this wandering preacher had become seriously unpopular) accompanies Joseph of Arimathea (J of A was quite someone – perhaps next year a play about him, Arthur, the Grail and Glastonbury? Let me know if you want more) and asks Pilate for the body of the crucified Jesus. That was rather brave; Pilate would have been very fed up with the whole thing by then and probably not too pleased to be disturbed again by these troublesome religious leaders. And it was rather brave because who knows what Caiaphas would say when he heard?

Nicodemus was probably quite rich, because he brought lots of expensive spices with him for the burial. For all those nervous, intelligent, hesitant, influential, rich people in the village, he might be a character of much interest. He was an honourable man.

All good wishes

Henry

# Letter 37

# Caiaphas, the danger
# of compromise

---

*September 1997*

Dear Major Quilter,

My fault - I should have explained: Caiaphas was the key player in that week in Jerusalem. He knew what he wanted, he was pulling the strings, he was balancing on a very difficult political tightrope and was generally very successful.

Until the Sunday morning, but that's another story.

He was responsible as High Priest for the orderly worship in the Temple, and that was the only job that really mattered in Jerusalem. The Romans had allowed him to be in this role since AD16. He was good at it, and his skills were especially needed in Passover week, when the place was full of pilgrims and tourists. And they were not only flocking to the Temple, they were remembering Moses and Liberation, new beginnings and freedom from tyranny. Caiaphas was adept at keeping good order, so the worshippers were content and the Romans did not get alarmed. The last thing he needed was a Moses-like figure appearing, talk of freedom, and Pharaoh-like figures being challenged.

And then Jesus comes riding in on a donkey, a kingly gesture. Not this week, Jesus, not Passover week. But he stays, and so Caiaphas decides he has to leave or has to die. But the crowds love him (he embodies hope), so he must be snatched secretly, quickly, at night. How to find him? A treacherous friend and thirty pieces of silver are enough.

Caiaphas ends up compromising his values and all that he is meant to stand for. He tries to get people to give concocted testimony, false witness, in the trial, and in doing so breaks one of the ten commandments (and if anyone should know those by heart, it is the High Priest). But from his point of view, the political necessities outweigh everything else. Jesus is too unpredictable, his claims too outrageous, the Romans too threatening, the crowds too large, for there to be any other option.

He plays a difficult hand with some skill, and apart from irritating Pilate (but they know each other well, and the irritation will pass) not much is lost. By Friday evening he would be relieved and grimly satisfied. And then comes Sunday morning, and all his plans and stratagems are overtaken by events.

All good wishes

Henry

# Letter 38

# Mary, the value of perseverance

*September 1997*

Dear Major Quilter,

Thank you for your letter. If there were to be a second figure 'not often mentioned at Easter' then perhaps Mary, the mother of Jesus, would be of interest (although any of the other Marys would be good). She is sometimes overlooked in those frenetic events of that first Easter Sunday, especially outside the Roman Catholic tradition, but her quiet perseverance was remarkable. From her obedient response to the angel's voice, to her pondering of all those strange visitors in Bethlehem and those strange words of Simeon in the Temple, to her feisty relationship with her son when he was grown up, to the unutterable agony of watching her son being crucified, she was there. She was there.

And later we hear of her being with the other disciples, waiting and praying in Jerusalem, still part of the team, still on the journey, still hopeful for the next step.

Hers is a remarkable story. Just think of it on the human level. It is complex and confusing enough being a parent in any circumstances, how much more when your son is Jesus?

Apologies for the brief letter. So much more that could be said but must dash now.

She was there.

That is the big thing. She was there. Always.

All good wishes

Henry

## Which people help, which people hinder?

All this about Easter – were these letters included because Henry wanted to intrigue me with the narrative? Mary of course I had heard of, Nicodemus and Caiaphas were new to me, and I admitted to myself that I was intrigued. I remembered his comment in an earlier letter about Christmas: begin by learning the story. And before those three there was the letter to his friend Mary, and gentle exploring of possible hurt received. There seemed to be something here about the power of individuals to help or harm an ongoing story.

The morning sun was now streaming through the windows, I glanced down at the box. Only a couple left.

# Letter 39

# A Farewell to Matilda

*January 1998*

Dear Matilda,

Thank you for your kind letter (never underestimate the gratitude of the elderly when the young take an interest!). You are very perceptive: you pick up so well how things are, but you do not fall in the trap of telling me what you think I should be feeling. I have had so much of that. The news was not a complete shock, I had sensed the lack of energy and spark for some time. So hard to put one's finger on it, and then the results explain it all.

Probably about six months, but could be shorter or longer.

In my usual idle and self-indulgent way, I have been considering how it all feels. Simple impending mortality, some might say, but we all know we are going to die. What is the difference between knowing I will die in the next fifty years (unless I break a few records) and knowing I will die this year?

Well, actually, rather a lot. But I am not quite sure why. Perhaps it is to do with knowing there are some things I will now never do. Or is it that life simply feels so rich and full that it seems strange that it might end? The party is still going on, why turn off the light?

All this musing has, I think, strengthened my belief in heaven. Yes, it might be wishful thinking, but I can't explain this feeling of life being 'cut short' except by thinking that life is meant to be more than our physical existence across a span of years. Were we nothing more than chemicals, I cannot see why death would feel like such an interruption.

Perhaps it would feel different if I were ninety-five.

What I want to do before I die is to thank people and say how much they mean to me, but I know I won't be able to do that adequately and sufficiently. I am increasingly aware that my energy levels will decline and there is less and less I will be able to do. But, at least I can make a start, so thank you Matilda, thank you so much. You have brought joy to me that I cannot express. If ever you need encouragement, remember that. Nothing that is done in love is ever lost or wasted. Be filled with hope that today you will change the world, as you have already changed mine.

Love

Henry

# Letter 40

# A challenge to James

_____

*June 1998*

Dear James,

You have reached the end. You were always patient with my ramblings. Thank you for reading them all through. I know you well enough, you would never turn straight to the end.

One final self-indulgent musing, just for you. Do you remember, as a teenager, telling me about your school weekend away? You talked about the importance for your little group to make the most of your map-reading skills, so as to progress over the hills, through the valleys, and finally to the campsite at the end of day.

Reaching the right destination involves agreeing where we are now (which will largely depend on our understanding of where we have come from), working out where we want to be, and deciding how we are going to get there. Those are the three questions that count.

What a map looks like depends on the priorities of the map-maker. A political map of the world is different to a physical map. A child's sketch of their walk to school, with particular places of interest listed, will be different to a council street-plan. What is placed at the centre of maps will vary, as one can see from mediaeval *Mappa Mundi* editions.

The desire to make maps, and to use maps, is perhaps part of our desire to place ourselves in some sort of context and to give some shape to the world around us. In the old days "Here be monsters" might occasionally have been written across areas outside the map-maker's knowledge, not because any had been seen there, but because this was a useful shorthand for "we don't know this part, and we all know how scary the unknown can feel."

James, ponder deeply what map you are using, who drew it, where you are on it presently (and how you got there) and where you want to go.

Enough of these cartographic conjectures! You may be wondering why I left these letters out for you. I think there are four reasons.

The first is simple, you have always meant a great deal to me, and if anyone is going to read these, I would like it to be you. You tend to underestimate how highly people think of you; James, I think the world of you and giving you these letters is a sign of trust. Through no fault of yours you were brought up in a context where there was much broken trust. It has taken you time to know that people can trust you and that you can trust others; so, if one of my last acts is to remind you how much I like and trust you, then I am content.

Secondly, I was not sure what to do with them! I do not really know why these kind people sent these back, which parts they found helpful and which were a hindrance. Perhaps that is true of all our words; we may be the worst judge of when we are being useful or not.

Thirdly, and this may sound rather intense as well, I wanted you to get to know me better, and reading someone's letters (especially knowing that they were not originally intended for your eyes) can be revealing. We have known each other for a long time, but I am a fairly private person. Looking at these again, I blush where I come over as rather pompous – and I am indeed a *very* amateurish poet!

And lastly, just possibly, there may be something here that is to do with hope. That is the common theme in this selection. Most of us struggle with hope; I think it would be helpful to you if you could find some more. We both know that your past has its particular complexities, that the present is confused, and the future is full of unknowns. Honour the past, do your best in the present, and be strong and positive about the future. That, dear James, is how it is. You are where you are and it is time to move forward. To face change with courage is a great sign of hope.

Do you remember what we used to say? How you heard each letter, James: "That says a lot about what you think of it."

I will stop now. Thank you for looking after these, whatever you decide to do.

May I call you my honorary great-nephew? That is how I always saw you.

With love

Henry

---

### An anticipated journey

I had been placing the letters face down. When I turned them back over, they were still in order, and it was easy to straighten them into a neat pile and replace them in the box.

I had learnt a little more about Henry, but there was much that was still hidden. There seemed to be a poignancy in some of these letters that I couldn't quite place. Some quiet research might be interesting.

And I had learnt a little more about myself, through my reactions to what I had read. There was more research I could do there, too.

*My guess is that you, James, will be the first person who sees this.*

I got up and stood in the doorway to the garden. I was glad I had come to the house. Even without Henry, the welcome was still here.

Part of the welcome was a kind of commissioning, a preparing for the next step. Henry was a shrewd handler of people, he would have known where that last sentence about being a great-nephew would take me. Profoundly moving, and profoundly challenging. I was grateful beyond words, whilst aware that if you are a member of the family, there are family duties to be done. That was a nice touch.

I wondered if I could find a way of contacting Matilda.

I would take the box with me and study the letters properly, but as the sun shone brightly on that spring morning I allowed the immediacy of some themes to stay with me. Had the confusion and fragilities of my early years been thieves of hope? And what might be the guardians of hope for me? In these letters I had sensed a voice of kindness, honesty and purpose. And of faith, about which I knew so little.

"The first person who sees this": If I am the first, then there will be others, and that can be my excuse for a book.

A book needs a title. Henry had said they were about hope, but there had also been much about courage in these letters. Courage to write, courage to keep going on, courage to face up to what was going on, courage to guide. And there was the reminder that truth sometimes needed more than prose, that poetry can be part of the story, and the memory that our choice of background music is a helpful guide to what we are truly thinking: "That says a lot about what you think of it." Above all they were *letters*, communications, a reaching out, to people in need. And I had read them as dawn was breaking, with all its promise of things becoming clear, of new beginnings and expectations, of colour and of light.

*Letters from Henry, songs for a brighter morning.*

A clumsy title, but it would do for now. And it would be a reminder to me of bright mornings on days that are not so pleasant. And it would be a reminder of someone who cared deeply for so many people, and for me, and who wanted me to hold on to hope, and not to let it go.

# Acknowledgements

Thank you to all those who have patiently read parts of the book and for their helpful and wise comments, especially my family, Monica, Frances, Richard and Katrina, and my dear colleague Gemma Birt. Especial thanks to Annie Bayley and Sarah Posner who then went through every word with grace and thoroughness and gave me much time and wisdom. And, as ever, to patient Philip Ralli at Highland Books. Everyone's guidance was invaluable, and of course the many remaining weaknesses are entirely my responsibility.

The G.K. Chesterton quotation in letter 8 is a poem called *Evening* from his private Notebook.

The C.S. Lewis quotation in letter 19 is from a letter of 19/04/1951 (C.S.Lewis *Letters*, Collins Fount Paperbacks 1988).

The poem *There may come a time* in letter 28 was originally written for the funeral of a young friend, Hamish, and is reproduced here by kind permission of his mother, Lucy.

Earlier versions of some of the other poems originally appeared in the author's "The King and the Storyteller" and "The Knights and the Table", published by New Generation Publishing